I0646408

The Embrace
in
Lenghu Town

Written by Yu Xiaotian

Illustrated by Zhai Yilin

New Classic Press

2024

NEW CLASSIC PRESS

Published by New Classic Press (UK) ★
5th Floor, 99 Mansell Street, London, E1 8AX, UK,
Great Britain ★ Established in the year 2008 ★
Seeking business opportunities worldwide

The Embrace in Lenghu Town

Original Title: 冷湖上的拥抱
Written by Yu Xiaotian
Illustrated by Zhai Yilin

Original Edition © Changjiang Children's Press (Group) Co., Ltd 2022
This English Edition Published in the United Kingdom of Great Britain and
Northern Ireland
by New Classic Press Limited in 2024

ISBN 978-1-917143-11-0

First printed in the United Kingdom of Great Britain and Northern Ireland

10 9 8 7 6 5 4 3 2 1

DESIGNED BY SRA BERKS

The publisher's policy is to use paper manufactured from sustainable forests.

CONTENTS

Chapter One

Qili[1] Town

---
1   Qili: "Qi" means seven. "Li" is a traditional unit of distance in China, generally considered to be approximately equivalent to 500 meters in modern measurements.

1

The "wall" went up in ten seconds, as yellow as mud.

The big "hand" that built it started by pushing it up and going through the protective forest. Poor, neat, and orderly poplar trees, their green tops blinked out in a flash. Then, with a big press down, the bossy yellow earth covered the whole small town. The hand didn't stop, rolling ahead like a big bulldozer. The blue sky and white clouds got less and less, pushed into a corner until they totally disappeared. Tall buildings and parks vanished in a second like they'd been squashed by giant feet.

The "hand" is the wind, the "wall" is the sand.

As the light got darker, Meng Haiyun looked out the window, her ears busy. The wind outside wasn't just wind; it was a big army stomping the land. The sand wasn't just sand; it was a big wave, a tsunami that, with a little pucker of the lips and a tilt of the neck, swallowed the small town.

Blimey, is this the end of the world?

Meng Haiyun's heart squeezed, her body stiff, but her eyes glanced outside. Her heart rose and fell with the wind and sand, slowly descending into chaos.

But ... why's everyone so calm?

The Maths teacher, Mr. Li, stood casually at the front, as if nothing had happened, teaching coordinates from the x-axis to the y-axis, finding where the lines crossed and marking a point. The whole classroom felt like a giant graph, with everyone busy at their points.

Finally, Mr. Li had a casual look out the window, closed the book, and said, "Time to go." Quick as a flash, lads packed their bags, carrying the bag in their hands or slinging it over their shoulders, saying, "See you, sir," and rushed out. Soon, people paired up and left, leaving Meng Haiyun behind.

Today was her first day in this school and class.

In the afternoon, when her class teacher, Ms. Huang, brought her here, she only had time to glance at the sign on the classroom door. Hmm, Class 5, 8th Grade. 5 didn't feel special, as 4 was her lucky number.

"Come up front and say hi to everyone," Ms. Huang led Meng Haiyun by hand to the front and gave her hair a stroke, causing her uneven fringe to bob up, "This hairstyle's in, isn't it? But it's covering your eyes. You should get it cut."

Meng Haiyun just tilted her head, avoiding Ms. Huang's hand, smiled, but with a firm tone, replied, "Nah."

The whole class burst into laughter. Even those who were whispering with lowered heads raised them. Everyone stared at her, making her feel like a new monkey in a zoo.

At this moment, the bell rang to her rescue. Meng Haiyun

secretly sighed in relief. Ms. Huang restored order, saying, "Let's start the class."

Actually, Meng Haiyun could tell that Ms. Huang was a good teacher. Her eyes had a slightly drooping corner, giving her face a touch of sadness, and her speaking tone was not strong. So, every word she said seemed to carry a bit of friendly advice. Meng Haiyun felt a bit guilty herself, but there was no other way. In this new place, she had to show all her "thorns" and ideally make them into armour, looking unapproachable for self-protection. She didn't know how long she'd stay in this damn place. Since she had no long-term plans for the future, she didn't want to show her soft side, nor did she want to make too many connections here. That way, when she left, it wouldn't be too sad.

Meng Haiyun has been sitting obediently and expressionless since the first class, neither answering questions nor interacting with her classmates around her, as if a statue had been airdropped into her seat, merely filling the space.

All afternoon, except for going to the toilet, she remained in this rigid posture. Her expression and muscles were tense, and she was actually very tired. When it came to the third class, "the end of the world" suddenly arrived; whether it was to rescue her or scare her, she was the only one perturbed in the whole classroom.

It was after packing her bag when Meng Haiyun suddenly

realised that she hadn't memorised the way from home to school. Her father had dropped her off at school in the afternoon, promising to pick her up after school. Now even if she went out, she couldn't go back home, only getting lost in the sandstorm. She couldn't help but panic. At that moment, someone tugged at her sleeve.

"Stop standing there, hurry up. I have to lock the classroom in a bit."

This was a girl wearing a checkered blouse under her school uniform, with short hair tied into a short plait. That plait was like a little tail, obediently hanging over her shoulder. When Meng Haiyun enrolled in the afternoon, Ms. Huang had introduced several class leaders to her, saying if there was anything, she could ask them for help. When pointing to a girl sitting in the back row, Ms. Huang was particularly proud, "That's our class monitor. I assigned a very difficult problem this morning, and they're all waiting for her to solve it."

Sure enough, that girl was surrounded by a crowd, like the moon surrounded by the stars, with some bowing their heads to look at her problem-solving process, and others holding her book to look at the notes inside. Through the crowd, Meng Haiyun only saw two pieces of checkered shirt collar flipped out, supporting her head.

"You're the class monitor, aren't you? What's your name again?"

"Du Yiming."

What a nice name! Outstanding people deserve good names, thought Meng Haiyun.

"Why was school suddenly dismissed?"

"Because a sandstorm is coming. We have sandstorm holidays in Dunhuang. Let's go home, and come back to class after the sandstorm."

Getting out of the door, Meng Haiyun realised how terrifying the sandstorm was. Unable to see the muddy and ugly face of this monster, she felt countless hands tearing at her. Clumps of sand and dust smashed into her face, each grain feeling solid, like sandpaper scraping her skin.

Du Yiming raised her collar to cover her mouth and half of her face, looking very experienced, and asked loudly, "Where do you live?"

"Uh, I ... I ... just a moment ..."

Meng Haiyun turned back, opened the notes on her mobile phone and had a quick glance at it, where her home address was written. She didn't want Du Yiming to think she was stupid. At her age, who wouldn't remember their home address! But she just couldn't. The home she remembered no longer existed.

"Home" isn't just an abstract idea. It's connected to every family member, dispersed in the daily life. Wherever you are, you always carry traces of home. It could also be said that a person's emotional blood is delivered by home. For Meng

Haiyun, her blood and heartbeat were given by her mother, and when her mother left, home disappeared.

"You're not very familiar with here, are you? Actually, this town isn't big, just a few streets." Du Yiming subtly dispelled her sadness.

Indeed, "it wasn't big", Meng Haiyun thought. The name Qili Town is quite common, many places across the country are called Qili Town or Shili Village. Qili Town also looked very ordinary, just a few intersecting streets. Walking here, one felt like stepping into a nostalgic art film: no 24-hour convenience stores, only old-fashioned small shops; no stylish salons, just the most ordinary barber shops; not even high-end restaurants, only the oilfield staff canteen built decently. Of course, everything here is related to oil. After all, this town is the office and living base of the Qinghai Oilfield. Oil Building, Oilfield News Centre, Oilfield Workers' Cultural Palace, Oilfield Digital Cinema, kindergartens, primary schools, middle schools ... everything you need. If willing, one could spend a lifetime here. The residential areas were concentrated, with uniform buildings, uniform layouts, with nodding machines[1] painted on the outer walls, and slogans.

Thinking about it, Meng Haiyun suddenly came to her senses: "Well, I just arrived, and I'm not familiar with everything

---

1 Nodding Machines, a type of machinery used in oil extraction. During operation, its movements resemble bowing, colloquially referred to as a "nodding machine."

here. Such a small place really isn't interesting. I'm from Hainan, where there's the sea. Have you ever seen the sea?"

"I haven't." Du Yiming remained calm, showing no sign of longing, and Meng Haiyun's somewhat deliberate sense of superiority vanished in an instant.

"I heard that many families here have several generations working in the oil fields. If it were me, even if they gave me tens of thousands every month, I wouldn't be able to endure it."

Du Yiming smiled lightly, calmly saying, "Maybe you won't think that way in the future."

Meng Haiyun suddenly understood why Ms. Huang liked this class monitor so much. She exuded a kind of calmness, confident yet not arrogant. She was like the ten-o'clock sun in spring, warm but not glaring, naturally casting her light on others. For example, at this moment, she volunteered to escort Meng Haiyun home, citing the reason that she might not find her way home.

2

As soon as Du Yiming entered Meng Haiyun's building, she noticed that Meng Haiyun lightened her steps, as if the stairs were fragile.

Cartoons on TV were playing loudly in the house, and a five or six-year-old girl was sitting in the middle of the floor, banging her toy ball onto the ground. Then, like a dart, a man shot towards where the ball landed, picked it up, and handed it back to the little girl. This was followed by a new round of throws ...

Meng Haiyun was a little surprised to see so many people at home.

"Dad, you're back early?"

"Yes, a sandstorm warning was issued today, so I brought Tongtong back early." Meng Haiyun's father, Meng Peng, said while gently handing the ball to the little girl.

"Oh."

Meng Haiyun felt a sudden pang in her chest, but couldn't say anything. So there was a sandstorm warning, so dad brought Tongtong back early, and she foolishly stayed in the classroom, scared half to death, it's really laughable.

"Hello, Mr Meng!"

Then, out of the blue, Du Yiming called from behind, and only then did Meng Haiyun remember that Du Yiming was still standing at the doorway. Seeing she had no intention of leaving, Meng Haiyun had to rummage through the messy pile of shoes and fetch a pair of slippers for her.

While handing over the slippers, Meng Haiyun quietly asked, "Aren't you going home?"

"During sandstorms, it's best not to be out. If you can't make it home, you have to find shelter nearby. My mum is probably stuck in the office right now, and I can't leave from your place."

"I wish we'd gone to your place today."

Meng Haiyun lowered her head to arrange the shoes they had changed out of. Her shoes were a pair of open-toed Mary Janes, quite common in Hainan, breathable to wear, but in Dunhuang, especially during sandstorms, wearing them was worse than going barefoot. Du Yiming's shoes were ankle-length boots, sealing her feet from the sand. Meng Haiyun stared at her own mismatched shoes and was lost in thought when suddenly she heard Du Yiming calling from behind, "Hello, sister."

Sister? Where did this sister come from in this family? Meng Haiyun lifted her head and saw Xiao Ge looking at them. She had just come out of the kitchen, rolling up her sleeves, hands still dripping with water, and upon hearing Du Yiming call her sister, she smiled.

"Oh, Haiyun brought a classmate home, come and take a seat please!"

The little girl, upon seeing Xiao Ge, raised her head and asked, "Mum, when are we eating?"

"Almost ready, darling. The chicken wings need to simmer a bit longer to get the flavour."

At this point, Meng Haiyun whispered, "Auntie."

Du Yiming immediately understood that Xiao Ge was Meng Haiyun's stepmother. Sensing the atmosphere becoming a bit awkward, she didn't say anything further.

Actually, children of oilfield workers often stayed overnight at classmates' homes. Du Yiming's situation was rather good: her mum worked in Dunhuang. Many classmates' parents worked in the distant Qaidam Basin and only returned to Dunhuang every two months when changing shifts; otherwise, they couldn't come back. These classmates were quite lonely, so they often stayed over at other classmates' homes. Since they were in the same class and lived close by, they would seize the opportunity to finish their homework together quickly and then play games or watch TV together. Their lives were generally simple and cheerful, as if programmed according to some routine. But Meng Haiyun wasn't part of this routine; she wasn't ready yet but was pushed into it. As an observer, Du Yiming stumbled upon the most secretive part of this family, which was a bit improper.

This home seemed perfect. The living room walls were painted Prussian blue, accentuating the white furniture and making it look clean and fresh. The bedroom wallpaper was covered in pink heart-shaped patterns, as if trying to envelop people in bubbles. Each room had a photo of three people— Meng Peng and Xiao Ge holding little Tongtong, forming a solid heart shape.

As soon as dinner was over, Meng Haiyun took Du Yiming to her bedroom. The bed in the bedroom was a bunk bed. Meng Haiyun first threw her backpack onto the lower bunk and sat down directly; then she remembered it was her sister's bed, jumped up, hit her head on the board of the upper bunk, and a few strands of hair got caught in the splinters. Annoyed, she shook her head, and a few strands of hair fell down. She grabbed her backpack and stuffed it into a basket in the corner, which seemed to be for holding dirty clothes, then smoothed out the lower bunk's bedsheet before pulling up a chair and sitting down.

"Do you sleep in this room with your sister?" Du Yiming quickly glanced around.

"Yes. This bed had been bought just before I came. Look, there are still new splinters here—" She pressed the edge of the bed with her fingers, feeling a bit sharp.

Du Yiming looked at the upper bunk, "If you sleep on

the lower bunk, I can squeeze in with you. But if it's the upper bunk, I'm afraid it might collapse with both of us on it."

Meng Haiyun tapped on the bed board and also felt it was a bit risky. "Then I'll sleep on the floor, there's a mat there." She pointed to a yoga mat rolled up in the corner.

"Then I'll sleep on the floor with you."

"Ha! Why? Diving into this mess with me?"

"Of course, if you jump, I'll jump too."

"Then you'll be miserable. We've only known each other for a day. Youhaven't tasted the sweet with me yet, but are already sharing my bitterness."

The two girls spread out the yoga mat, used blankets as mattresses, and pillows as headrests, leaning against the wall. A piece of wallpaper fell off the wall with a snap, and they both looked up to see that the wallpaper had cracked, with old wall plaster bulging inside, choosing this moment to peel off.

Meng Haiyun held up the piece of wallpaper to look at it, then turned to Du Yiming and asked, "Aren't you curious about our family?"

It seemed like all the stories were just waiting for an outlet, and now they finally burst forth.

Meng Haiyun's dad, Meng Peng, was an oilfield child who grew up in a town called Lenghu in Qinghai. This town was at the foot of the Kunlun Mountains, surrounded by deserts; besides mountains, there was only sand. Sometimes, when standing on a slightly higher sand dune and looking around, one could only see endless yellow sand in all directions. Lenghu was originally an uninhabited area, but in the 1950s, oil was discovered, attracting tens of thousands of oil workers and their families. Houses, restaurants, schools, and drilling rigs were built like stacked blocks on the desert; pump jacks dotted the land, stretching out in a continuous line on this land; oil tankers, like ants, sketched out winding oil transportation tracks in the desert. This endless desert was like a big piece of monotonous blanket, with the only pattern being the small sand dunes with various shapes and sizes peculiar to deserts: tall, short, big, small, resembling humans, resembling animals, crouching, leaping, fuzzy, or menacing ... There wasn't even a tree around, only a kind of grass called camel thorn flying in tufts with their rough tangled hair. So every day he wondered when he could leave this monotonous place and see what was written in those books, such as towering trees, boundless oceans, and bustling cities.

My dad finally graduated from high school, and my grandpa insisted he apply to Petroleum University. My dad did apply and got in, but once he graduated, he secretly went to Hainan to do business and met a Hainanese girl there, whom he married and had a child with—that's me," Meng Haiyun pointed to herself.

"What happened next? How's your mum doing now? Why did you leave her and come here?" Du Yiming asked.

Meng Haiyun grabbed the pillow behind her, buried her head in it, and her voice was muffled when she spoke again.

"What's wrong? Feeling sleepy already?" Du Yiming nudged Meng Haiyun's armpit.

Most people would have either started fidgeting or laughed uncontrollably, but Meng Haiyun neither moved nor laughed. She lifted her head, pursed her lips, her voice low and fragmented.

"They separated when I was a child. My mum passed away in a car accident recently. Do you know? That morning, I didn't even say 'goodbye' to her," Meng Haiyun paused for a second or two, "Now, no matter how much I regret it, it's useless."

Du Yiming didn't expect it to be like this. She pulled out a tissue and handed it to Meng Haiyun, but seeing Meng Haiyun lower her head without responding, she had to use it herself. "Luckily, you still have your dad," she said.

"Dads can never replace mums, you know that," Meng Haiyun replied.

Just then, Meng Haiyun heard faint footsteps outside the door, and then the door was pushed open. Meng Peng stuck his head in, took a look, then tiptoed in, lowering his voice as he said, "Sis is sleeping on Mum's bed today, and I am bringing her blanket over. Don't mind me, carry on with your chat."

After saying that, Meng Peng picked up the space-cotton blanket from the lower bunk. The cloud-like blanket obstructed his view, and he stumbled towards the door, almost hitting the doorframe. Du Yiming thought of helping him, but he waved his hand and pointed at Meng Haiyun, then retreated out of the door, casting a glance at Meng Haiyun before finally closing it.

"Your dad actually cares a lot about you."

"Does he? In this family, I'm redundant. I'm only unique to Mum, but Mum is gone ..." Meng Haiyun's lips trembled slightly, her mouth curved downward, her face swaying like a shaken satin ribbon with rhythmic pulsations, her eyes shimmering with mercury-like tears—tears falling down just like that.

The tissue was already crumpled from earlier use. Du Yiming had to use her hand to wipe off Meng Haiyun's tears. As soon as she touched Meng Haiyun's skin, it felt like she was scalded. Her skin was smooth and soft, like tofu. Southern girls indeed have great skin! She thought to herself.

"Stop crying, you won't be beautiful if you cry more"

Although that's what she said, Meng Haiyun was always beautiful, tears on her were like moonlight on water.

"I'm not crying. Anyway, my grandma said if I can't stand it anymore, I can go back to Hainan. She'll take care of me."

Meng Haiyun lowered her head like a closed flower. Du Yiming quickly let her lean on her shoulder. That fringe, praised by Mrs. Huang as "in trend", lightly trembled with her breath. She didn't change her position for a while. Du Yiming called her softly a couple of times before realizing she had fallen asleep.

That night, Meng Haiyun dreamed of a whale, her favourite ocean creature. The whale drifted from south to north in the air, like a huge submarine, cruising between the desert and the sky. She rode on the whale, their shadows covering the earth like an umbrella. But soon, a demonic wind arose from the ground, spinning and rushing, the sand dust rising like hissing snakes, spiraling higher than them, descending upon them like a torrential rain. Meng Haiyun's little world, like a breached trench, was filled with sand in every crevice. But was it sand? It flowed more than water, colder than ice, more ferocious than the sea, filling every pore, carving pits in her heart and lungs. She shouted in despair, "Mum, mum ..." but as soon as she opened her mouth, sand poured in, and she couldn't say a word. At that instant, the whale collapsed like a sand dune, and she fell straight down with it.

Meng Haiyun felt like she had hit the ground, trembling violently, waking up in a cold sweat. After a few seconds, she realized her back was firmly against the bed board. So, it was the bed. Oh, wait, wasn't she sleeping on the floor yesterday?

She got up and looked around, noticing the mess on the floor had been cleared up, the yoga mat rolled back to its original place. She climbed down and saw Du Yiming sleeping on the upper bunk. She guessed Du Yiming had her father move her to the lower bunk and cleaned up the mess on the floor before climbing up to sleep. What a considerate girl.

She drew the curtains but couldn't tell if the sandstorm had stopped. Out of the window was all brown. Brown particles squeezed the sky, leaving no room for the sun. Meng Haiyun wished she could fit the Hainan sun into her eyes, to bring it out whenever she wanted. She pushed the window open, a strong, dry sand smell immediately filled the room, making it hard to breathe. She spread her fingers, attempting to peel off this layer of sand curtain outside. But she couldn't move this invisible yet heavy curtain, so she waited, for this city to "shake off" the sand itself to give her a clearer view.

Dunhuang wasn't just a city's name, it was also a huge exclamation mark on the Silk Road. But during her visit these days, only the taste of sand remained as an exclamation mark in her mind.

Meng Haiyun heard slight movements outside the room, like someone dragging a suitcase. Soon after, toothbrushing sounds came from the bathroom, she could tell it was her father from the rhythm of spitting water. After living here for a few days, she had figured out everyone's toothbrushing rhythm. Dad woke up so early?

Meng Haiyun opened the door and tiptoed out, her dad's suitcase was in the hallway. It was quite old, with peeling corners and seams.

Meng Peng was startled to see her and asked, "Why are you

That night, Meng Haiyun dreamed of a whale, her favourite ocean creature. The whale drifted from south to north in the air, like a huge submarine, cruising between the desert and the sky. She rode on the whale, their shadows covering the earth like an umbrella.

up so early?"

"Can't sleep. Are you going on another business trip?"

"Yeah, I need to go to the south to get some equipment, the oil field urgently needs it."

Meng Peng was a buyer in the equipment department, often travelling far and wide, comparing prices and quality, striving to provide the oil field with the best value equipment.

Going to the south?

For Meng Haiyun, the south was a beautiful place. There was no sandstorm, only moist air and the sweet scent of coconut. More importantly, it held the memories of the brief warm moments spent with her family.

However, for Meng Haiyun, the south was also a difficult choice, with the other option being the northwest desert her father couldn't let go of. Whenever young Meng Haiyun demanded her father's attention, her mother always said, "When grandma gets better, dad will come back." Now she realised, like herself, her father was also facing a dilemma—between his parents and his wife and daughter.

Although her father's choice seemed obvious, she still wanted to ask him, "Do you miss Mum?" This question lingered on Meng Haiyun's mind for a long time, but she couldn't ask directly, and she felt distant from her father over the years, not close enough to share everything.

Countless words were stuck in her throat, but she couldn't

utter a single one. All her thoughts flowed to her fingers and toes through her blood. All her fingers and toes pointed towards her father, screaming at him, but he couldn't hear.

Meng Haiyun picked up her suitcase and bag from the floor and said, "Dad, let me see you off."

Every windowsill on each floor's corridor was piled high with thick sand, as if the building was being buried. Though the windows were tightly closed, sand still found its way in. People felt like insects sealed in a bottle, half-buried in sand. Only on the third floor's windowsill, something was sparkling. Perhaps it was a brooch someone had placed there. Coming from the warm and moist Hainan to Dunhuang, Meng Haiyun was impressed most by the dryness. Her skin felt tightened, her throat and nostrils felt dry, she felt like a fish thrown ashore.

In a moment of intense emotion, like a thirst for water, she decided to ask the pressing question. As she lifted her head, she saw her father looking at her too.

"What's wrong?"

"Dad, do you regret it?"

Meng Peng was initially puzzled, but quickly understood. He avoided her gaze, then chuckled helplessly and changed the subject, "Haiyun, your grandfather is coming in a few days. Xiao Ge needs to take care of your sister, so you'll have to look after your grandfather."

Then he took the bag and swung it onto his back, saying,

"You may go back now, no need to see me off."

After that moment of closeness, they became polite yet distant again. She stood still, not offering to accompany him further, listening to her father's footsteps growing fainter. She rarely had the chance to listen to that sound because there were always too many unresolved issues between her and her father—sometimes time, sometimes distance, sometimes other people ...

Du Yiming was speaking on the phone in a low voice, and when she saw Meng Haiyun return, she quickly said, "Mum, I'll hang up ... Alright, I'll have breakfast, don't worry too much, you'll get grey hairs."

After she hung up, Meng Haiyun asked, "Where did your mum sleep yesterday?"

"She got stuck in the office and had to sleep on the desk. She used a mop cloth to block the window gaps, but guess what? When she woke up, there was a human shape on the table, surrounded by sand."

"They still have to use cloths to block the window gaps? Why didn't we do that yesterday?"

"We used to do that a few years ago; aluminum alloy doors and windows are prone to deformation from the pressure of sand. It's been better since we switched to plastic steel windows these years. Your house has plastic steel windows, but my mum's office still has aluminum alloy windows."

"Isn't there a protective forest? Isn't it effective?"

"It is, for normal sandstorms, the protective forest works well. But when the sandstorm is too severe, layer after layer of sand piles up, and the protective forest can't stop it."

"Oh, so it's like this here all the time?"

"It'll get better after the eighth day of the fourth lunar month." Du Yiming remembered something and chuckled, "There's a place nearby called Gaolaozhuang. People say things will improve when Zhu Bajie[1] gets married. By the way, did you go out? What's it like outside?"

"Looks like the sandstorm has eased a bit, don't know if we can go to school."

"Let me check." Du Yiming crawled down from the upper bunk, pulled back the curtains and looked outside, "Hmm, according to my experience ..." She deliberately drew out her words, then turned back with a serious face. Seeing Meng Haiyun's nervous and expectant look, she burst into laughter, "We can go to school."

The two girls got ready for school, opened the door, and saw Xiao Ge helping Tongtong get dressed. Tongtong was very cute, with rounded features, chubby arms and legs, and a slight downward curve at the corners of her eyes, making her look very innocent. So even when she emptied the bowl of mushrooms and broccoli onto the floor, even when she banged on the bed with her toys at night to make Meng Haiyun play with her,

---

1   Zhu Bajie: a major character of the 16th century Chinese novel *Journey to the West*.

Meng Haiyun couldn't get angry with her. Because whenever Meng Haiyun glared at her, she would smile brightly and call out in a childish voice, "Sis—sis—"

Xiao Ge was fumbling with Tongtong's buttons, but every time she buttoned one, Tongtong would unbutton another. As she patiently buttoned up again, she kept an eye on the milk in the pot. It had been boiling with froth for a while.

"I need to get to work early today. Can you dress yourself?"

"No ... I ... can't ..."

It wasn't until Meng Haiyun rushed into the kitchen to turn off the stove and poured the milk, which had formed a skin on top, into a bowl, that Xiao Ge's eyes showed a bit of warmth.

Meng Haiyun suddenly felt encouraged and couldn't help but ask Xiao Ge, "Do you want me to take my sister to kindergarten? It's on the way."

Yesterday when she returned, she happened to pass by the kindergarten. The kindergarten, primary school, and middle school were all close by. In other places, completing one's education often meant travelling across half the city, but in Qili Town, from entering kindergarten to finishing middle school, it only required crossing two blocks.

Xiao Ge hesitated for a moment and said, "No need, no need. You also need to go to school, don't be late." Meng Haiyun didn't say anything more.

After the sandstorm, Dunhuang was filled with sandbags

everywhere, with a uniform earthy colour and extremely rough texture. But seen from a distance, clear layers were visible, giving it a beauty reminiscent of landscape paintings from Song Dynasty.

Du Yiming looked around and said, "It's like this down here, but we can't be sure what it's like up there."

"What do you mean by down here and up there?"

"Oh, I forgot you still don't understand these things. Down here refers to Dunhuang; up there refers to Huatugou. Huatugou is the front line of Qinghai Oilfield. My dad works up there. They change shifts and come back to Dunhuang every two months, right? They call it 'going down'; and when they return to the oilfield, they say 'going up.' People here always ask, 'Have you come down?' or 'Are you going up again?' Don't act like you don't understand."

"I still don't get it. Why is Huatugou called 'up' there?"

"Because it's at a high altitude, around two or three thousand metres. A journalist once said, the people up there is already making contribution just by lying in bed, not to mention they have to do oil drilling."

"Then what about Lenghu? Why do I remember Lenghu as the oil extraction base?" Meng Haiyun had a deep impression of the name Lenghu. It was because her mother was defeated by the terrifying altitude sickness after visiting Lenghu, which led to her father being torn between the south and the north.

"Lenghu is the old oil extraction base. According to my mum, after oil was discovered, many people moved to Lenghu with their families, forming a small town of tens of thousands. But later, the oil there gradually dried up, and the place became deserted. After the discovery of Huatugou Oilfield, the oil extraction base was relocated there, and the administrative base moved to Dunhuang."

"What does Lenghu look like now?"

"Why are you so curious about Lenghu? I've never been there, but my mum said there are all collapsed houses now. It looks very dilapidated, with nothing left."

3

Meng Haiyun's grades were passable at her previous school, but here, she just couldn't get into the study groove and often found herself daydreaming in class. One day, as she was doodling absentmindedly, her teacher, Mr. Li, asked the students to answer questions in sequence. When it was her turn, Li tapped her desk and asked what she was doing. She instinctively stood up, glanced at her notebook, and realised she had unconsciously written the words "Lenghu," with hollow shadows underneath. At first glance, those two words seemed to be trembling. There were also various doodles around them—a broken heart, a stack of burning letters, a flying apsaras ...

Mr. Li glanced at her and said, "Are you sleepwalking? Sit down, you need to pay attention in class!"

The other students smoothly picked up Li's sequential questioning. The classroom was like this, a brief disorder was like ripples on the water's surface, spreading instantly and soon disappearing. However, the ripples in Meng Haiyun's heart couldn't be smoothed out for a long time.

Before coming to Dunhuang, Meng Haiyun only knew that

it was an important stop on the Hexi Corridor, and the Hexi Corridor and the Silk Road were unfamiliar terms in geography books, unrelated to herself. History here was stacked like sand, with dynasties changing like punctuation marks on a long scroll. She used to think that standing on this land would bring her closer to history, but when she actually arrived, she found that all cities looked different on the surface, but life was the same everywhere. She naively thought that the schools in the oil fields would teach them some knowledge related to oil, but they didn't. Even the people working in the oil fields seemed to care only about their children's entrance exams, never expecting the children to understand their work.

After maths class was the class break for physical exercises. Ms. Huang came in to urge everyone, standing at the door waving her arms, "Go out and do exercises, don't just stay in the classroom!"

A pile of light blue uniforms with dark blue stripes swayed on the field. The students, wearing loose-fitting uniforms, stood in loose lines, raising their hands and kicking, weak and powerless, resembling a pile of inflatable human-shaped balloons, without bones, barely standing.

Since Meng Haiyun was new and didn't have a fixed spot, it felt strange wherever she stood. So Du Yiming pulled her to stand in front of her, where no one would object.

The preparation music was the theme song of the

documentary "Hexi Corridor," called "Dream of the Hexi Corridor." As soon as it started playing, Meng Haiyun felt like the sky and earth had suddenly disappeared, and everything around her rapidly receded, becoming vast and empty. At this moment, she was standing on the Hexi Corridor leading to the Western Regions, surrounded by flowing history.

It was the flourishing Tang Dynasty. Buzzing noises filled her ears, various languages from different countries, was it in the marketplace? Monks, merchants, dancers, commoners ... Here, languages from all over naturally blended together, unfamiliar accents with a prosperous atmosphere. The bustling crowd appeared as tiny dots from her vantage point. The city was like a flower blooming in the desert, where people lived and worked, thriving endlessly. Countless streets crisscrossed, forming a prosperous network of towns and counties.

Meng Haiyun felt like her vision couldn't encompass everything. The wind had blown gently for thousands of years, warm and delicate, with a slightly bitter "nasal tone", carving out countless yardang landforms, magnificent and grand.

The place where she stood seemed to be divided into two halves, one modern and one ancient, and she was like a pit in the middle. The worlds on both sides were gradually extending, rotating and shifting, until finally returning to calm.

The wind, like a hand, passed through the ages, caressing Meng Haiyun's bangs. Her scalp tingled a bit, but the next moment, her scalp felt like it's exploding, and her consciousness returned.

She heard someone ask in a displeased tone, "Who are you?"

4

Meng Haiyun had a special ability to switch emotions and expressions at any time, like a chameleon. For example, when she was at school, she would put on a stern face, displaying an expression completely unrelated to her surroundings; but once she returned home, she would reveal all her sensitivity and softness. This was a strategy.

So when she saw Yu Junying, her first impression was that the person in front of her might be employing the same strategy as her, because they looked so alike.

Meng Haiyun saw a fair-skinned boy, with no spots or bloodshot on his face, tall and slim, with elegant bone structure. His short hair, neat and fluffy, covered his perfectly curved head, accentuating his smooth and full forehead. He wore a white hoodie, half covering his head with the hood. The white colour complemented his handsome appearance, even adding a hint of luster. He gave off an aura of coldness and aloofness, to the extent that Meng Haiyun was surprised when she heard his slightly immature voice. Upon closer inspection, she noticed that he was wearing braces, causing his speech to be slightly unclear.

Someone nearby teased,

"Yu Junying, you're back late, someone else took your place."

"Du Yiming doesn't care about you anymore!"

The boy turned around and retorted to the teaser, "Shut up!"

Du Yiming quickly stepped forward to explain, "This is Meng Haiyun, the new student in our class. I saw that she had nowhere to stand, so I let her stand here first. You can find another spot."

The boy didn't say anything further and obediently found another place. After he left, Du Yiming asked, "Hey, weren't you supposed to come back in a week?"

The boy waved his hand, making a gesture to discuss it later.

It's curious, Meng Haiyun thought, this boy who seemed so distant, who was just growling at her a moment ago, was now constrained by Du Yiming's words.

After the exercises, Yu Junying took the initiative to walk back to Du Yiming's side and took out his phone, shaking it, "I took a lot of photos up there, want to see?"

Meng Haiyun heard clearly that Yu Junying said "up there." Du Yiming mentioned "up there" referring to the oil field. So, did he just return from the oil field? At the mention of the oil field, Meng Haiyun became interested.

Du Yiming's eyes lit up, "Quick, let's take a look!"

Meng Haiyun also approached. However, Yu Junying said, "Wait a moment, I need to go potty."

Meng Haiyun raised her head, somewhat surprised that Yu Junying used such a girly term for going to the restroom. It wasn't until she saw Yu Junying walk into the women's restroom that she understood.

"How did he ... how did he enter the women's restroom?"

"Oh my God!" Du Yiming's eyes widened, her smile growing bigger and bigger until she couldn't help but bend over laughing, her shoulders shaking, "Yu Junying is a girl!"

"Huh?"

The people around them also burst into laughter, including students from other classes. Meng Haiyun turned to them and asked, "Did you all know?"

Meng Haiyun was still trying to wrap her head around it. She wondered, would Yu Junying, with her stern little face and boyishly slender figure, blush if wearing a skirt? Well, if she did blush, it might make her look a bit cuter.

"Was she always like a boy since she was little?" Meng Haiyun was very curious.

"Yes, it's said that she was." Du Yiming said.

"Are you two close? She seems quite rebellious."

"One day, when we were doing exercises, I was chatting

with another girl. Yu Junying was between us. At that moment, Ms. Huang walked over, and the other girl stopped talking. Ms. Huang thought I was talking to Yu Junying, so she made the two of us stand outside for punishment."

"It was a total disaster! She should hate you for that, right?"

"I thought she would hate me too, but who knows what she was thinking. Anyway, we became friends after that."

There was a bang, and it turned out to be Yu Junying coming out of the women's restroom, kicking away a soccer ball that was rolling towards her. She shook the water off her hands and adjusted her hat. This time, Meng Haiyun, Du Yiming, and another girl from Class Three all smiled at her together.

"What are you laughing at?" Yu Junying walked over, looking at the three of them inexplicably.

"We're laughing at you," the girl from Class Three answered eagerly.

Yu Junying immediately understood what was going on and rolled her eyes, "Childish!"

Yu Junying brought her phone in front of Du Yiming, and the two of them leaned in together, whispering as they scrolled through the phone.

Meng Haiyun heard intermittent conversations, "This is Kunlun Mountains, this one is where my dad works ... Oh, that one, that's ..."

Meng Haiyun interjected, "That's a little fox."

It turned out she couldn't resist leaning in earlier. Yu Junying discreetly shifted the phone, and Meng Haiyun ended up standing in a position where she couldn't see the screen clearly due to the reflection.

Meng Haiyun wasn't annoyed; she turned to Du Yiming. "Yiming—," she said dejectedly, "she won't let me see." Then she pointed at Yu Junying.

Yu Junying furrowed her brows. "I didn't intend to show you."

"What harm would it do to let me see? There is nothing to lose for you." Meng Haiyun tugged at Du Yiming's sleeve. "Yiming, can you persuade her for me?"

Fortunately, Du Yiming wasn't wearing glasses; otherwise, they might have fallen off because of surprise. It turned out that Meng Haiyun would also laugh in school, but it was fleeting, sometimes tinged with a hint of sarcasm. Her most common expression was tilting her face upward. Because of her slightly upturned nose, when she tilted her face, her nose and lips formed an upward curve, giving her a somewhat proud look. But after their previous interactions, Du Yiming felt that Meng Haiyun just had something on her mind, so she pretended to be a "hedgehog" herself.

Du Yiming said to Yu Junying, "Let her see, please."

Yu Junying snorted and moved the phone slightly towards Meng Haiyun, accepting Meng Haiyun begrudgingly for Du

Yiming's sake.

"It's really beautiful. Were all these photos taken up there?" With each slide of the photos, Meng Haiyun exclaimed in admiration, mimicking the locals by referring to the oil field as "up there."

Yu Junying couldn't stand this exaggerated praise, showing a conflicted expression of half disdain and half reluctance, reluctantly responding with an "hmph."

"Don't you need to go to school?"

"My mum asked a special leave for me."

"That's nice!"

Meng Haiyun's voice sounded slightly downcast, which Yu Junying didn't notice, but Du Yiming did. She quickly changed the subject, "What did you guys write about in the composition class just now? It was so difficult!"

Yu Junying didn't pay any attention and continued, "I only see her once every two months, so she owes me."

Yu Junying's mother was a flight attendant, and her father worked at the oil field. Both of them worked on a schedule where they alternated every two months. Perhaps they had agreed early on to either come home together or not at all. While there were many children of double-income families in the oil field, most of them still had elderly relatives to take care of them. Yu Junying was an exception, relying entirely on herself. No matter how late she came home, whether she did her homework or how she performed in exams, no one cared. Both sets of grandparents lived far away and couldn't come to QiLi Town. The adults all felt guilty about this child. Whenever they called, they started with, "Ying, what gift do you want?" Later on, they didn't even need to call; Yu Junying called them herself, and could get four times the money to buy one thing— one from each parent, and one from each set of grandparents. Finally, it was Ms. Huang who personally called Yu Junying's mother, saying that it couldn't go on like this, there couldn't be no adults at home all the time. So, when her mother returned home once again, she took Yu Junying with her. Wherever her mother went, Yu Junying went too. Ms. Huang was also unhappy about this, saying that Yu Junying would fall behind in her studies this way. So, they changed it to Yu Junying accompanying her mother for a week every two months. Yu Junying had been to many places, such as Lanzhou, Qingdao, Shenzhen, and Beijing, all on her mother's regular flight routes. However, her impressions of these places were simple; they were just airports. She would take a stroll around the airport, buy some local specialties, look at the local tourist advertisements, and consider it the end of her journey to the city. Occasionally, her mother would take her to go "up there" to see her father, but the conditions "up there" were too poor, and both mother and daughter disliked it, so the number of visits was rare.

A few days ago, it was one of those rare visits. "Up there"

was still uninteresting, but the surprise came from her encounter with a little fox.

For Yu Junying, the days of going to school were well-organised, she just need to follow the routine; but the days without school were chaotic. She would lie down for a while, then do homework, then check her mobile phone, then order takeout, until she fell asleep in her clothes. During the weekend, Yu Junying didn't brush her teeth or wash her face; she would only clean up when she had to go to school. That was until she met Du Yiming ...

After showing the photos, Yu Junying took back her phone and casually set a close-up of a snowy mountain she took as the wallpaper.

The snow-capped mountains were embedded in the sky, forming winding silhouettes, with wind turbines poking into the bottom, creating a unique and elegant landscape. Meng Haiyun had never seen snow-capped mountains before, so she watched with particular attention.

Yu Junying looked up and met a pair of eyes filled with admiration. She didn't know that this snowy mountain had struck a chord of wind chimes in Meng Haiyun's heart.

When Meng Haiyun was sorting through her mother's belongings after her mother's death, she found a letter her father had written to her mother. At that time, her father was still deeply in love with her mother. During his summer vacation from university, he looked out over Kunlun Mountain and Qilian Mountain from afar and wrote, "The mountains are vast and white, and the snow on the mountaintops is glistening. Sliding down along the slope, it's a beautiful sight."

There was another lineof her mother's handwriting, "How could there be snow in August? Fabricated lies!"

It turned out that her mother was actually wrong; in some places in the Kunlun Mountains and Qilian Mountains, there was snow all year round. Growing up by the sea in the south, her mother had seen the vast expanse of the ocean, but had no imagination for the mountains wandering among the clouds— Perhaps there had been cracks between her father and her mother since then?

Oh, the distant, distant snowy mountains; the distant, distant Lenghu.

5

In the office, Ms. Huang was correcting compositions, and when she got tired, she picked up her mug and sipped coffee. Soon, she noticed another person beside Du Yiming on the field. Yu Junying and Meng Haiyun stood on her left and right, looking like a pair of guardian angels.

"They actually get along well?" She originally thought that with Yu Junying back, Meng Haiyun would be left alone again.

At this moment, another teacher said, "It's probably Du Yiming's credit! Who doesn't like such a girl?"

Yes, everyone loves Du Yiming. She was like a clean and tidy room, with warm decorations, warm, comfortable, attracting everyone to stay with her consistent hospitality and moderate tranquility. But from time to time, Ms. Huang cast her gaze towards Meng Haiyun, who seemed like a castle built of stones, standing alone there, with frosted glass windows and tightly drawn curtains, making it difficult to find the entrance even if you walked around the castle.

The topic she assigned for the recent in-class essay was "Reflections."

Almost without exception, the students wrote about stories around them, such as teachers' care, parents' kindness, and classmates' mischief. Only one composition caught her attention, which began like this:

"*Lonely smoke rises in the vast desert, the setting sun dyes the frost. The flying sleeves dance lightly, the sound of camel bells is long and melodious. Loulan has a history of thousands of years, vast and boundless. Beyond the Yangguan Pass, old friends have disappeared. On the Jiayu Pass, I hold a clear breeze and bright moon. By the crescent spring, I warm a bowl of longing for home. People hesitate on the road westward, looking back at the maple leaves of Jiangnan turning yellow. Thousands of miles of wind and sand, when will autumn end and return to the hometown? When the rain in Jiangnan stops, the Hexi Corridor stretches far. Amidst the sounds of flutes and pipes, snow falls heavily with sorrow.*"

She quickly flipped to the cover and found that it was written by Meng Haiyun.

Wow, this girl unexpectedly had such literary talent? She asked Du Yiming in private, and Du Yiming said that Meng Haiyun didn't quite like it here and had always thought about going back to Hainan to find her grandmother if she couldn't get used to it.

Don't be fooled by the apparent indifference of Meng Haiyun. In fact, she was more sensitive than local children and could feel the uniqueness of this land better.

So, would her experiences here open her heart? Or would her heart's door open at the knock of friendship?

Young Ms. Huang pondered. Day by day, she was being eagerly watched by dozens of pairs of eyes, and gradually, the door of Classroom Five became her heart's door. Whenever she took a brief rest like this, this heart's door became a mirror, reflecting the figure of each student clearly. She could see their colourful inner worlds, some blue, some warm yellow, some turning white at times, some turning grey at times. She cherished every child and wanted to protect the colours of their inner worlds. She just wanted to accompany them and watch them grow day by day.

In the next moment, she laughed at herself, feeling like an old bird protecting its chicks. The chicks seemed to be unchanged day by day, but upon closer inspection, they had grown a few ounces.

Chapter Two

Dangjin Mountain

1

The journey home was too short. After school, Meng Haiyun had to come up with all sorts of ways to kill time on the way home: stepping out with her left foot first, then her right foot; if the order was wrong, she'd go back and start again. She mentally gridded the road, stepping on only one square at a time, which slowed her pace on the way home.

Since her father went on a business trip, she came home even later. At first, she wanted to continue her habit from Hainan, which was to rinse the rice and add a finger-section's depth of water to cook it, then start her homework when the rice cooker began to work. But she made a mistake on her first try. The more careful she was, the more she couldn't get it right. The rice ended up half-cooked, like an apple with half of it worm-eaten, leaving people unsure whether to eat it or throw it away. She used to cook rice very well, soft and moist with some holes, and the air danced like elves inside. This unexpected mistake made her very frustrated. But what made her even more frustrated was Xiao Ge's indifferent attitude. Rice was not served for dinner; instead, noodles were served.

Meng Haiyun couldn't bear it and said to Xiao Ge, "Auntie, I cooked rice."

"Oh, that rice wasn't cooked properly. Don't eat it, save it for porridge tomorrow morning. Your sister only eats noodles and doesn't like rice. If you're craving rice, you can make a portion just for yourself in the future."

Feeling a bit lost, Meng Haiyun ate a few bites of noodles and then put down her chopsticks. She wanted to wash her bowl and chopsticks in the kitchen, but Xiao Ge told her to leave them in the sink.

There was a burnt smell in the air, and Meng Haiyun suddenly remembered that she hadn't unplugged the rice cooker, and the bottom of the pot was burnt.

"Auntie, the rice is burnt, what should we do?"

"I'll deal with it later."

Tongtong walked into the kitchen at some point and threw the spoon on the ground with a bang, splashing oil and vegetables all over the floor. Xiao Ge sternly scolded, "You're not a baby anymore, why do you still need Mum to feed you!"

Tongtong was frightened by her mother's sudden scolding and started crying. Meng Haiyun was about to go over and hug her sister, when suddenly, there was a knocking sound at the door. Xiao Ge said, "It might be the neighbour," and quickly ran to open the door.

Immediately, Meng Haiyun heard Xiao Ge apologizing

repeatedly, "Dad? Oh, I'm sorry, I forgot to pick you up at the station. It's all my fault!"

She saw Xiao Ge coming in carrying a large colourful woven bag, the kind often seen in the hands of old men picking up paper boxes on the roadside. Immediately after, a grey-haired, dark-skinned old man came in panting heavily. Meng Haiyun suddenly remembered that before going on his business trip, her father had told her that her grandfather was coming.

The old apartment building was low-rise and had no elevator, so climbing the stairs was definitely a big challenge for the elderly. Meng Haiyun hadn't seen her grandfather for several years. She had a photo of her grandfather, who was serving in the army when he was young, on her phone. After many years, the person in front of her didn't match the one on the photo. Grandpa's face was wide and flat, with a thin nose, as if the dough had been rolled into thin strips and stuck on the face. She looked at him and remembered the young and spirited soldier in the photo, but for a moment, she couldn't reconcile the two.

Grandpa was exhausted, sitting down heavily on Tongtong's small chair, and then quickly unbuttoning his shirt. There was a small triangular area of dark red skin under his neck, distinctly darker than the surrounding skin, showing that he didn't usually wear this turtleneck shirt. After unbuttoning his shirt, his breathing became a bit more regular. Leaning against the narrow, pink backrest of the chair, he lowered his head, his breath carrying a sturdy yet simple, elderly scent.

Grandpa's name was Meng Qingshan. After his wife passed away, he didn't want to burden his son anymore, so he went back to his hometown in Tianshui with the excuse of returning to his roots. This time, he heard that Meng Haiyun was attending school in Dunhuang, so he came to see his elder granddaughter as soon as possible.

Xiao Ge hurried into the kitchen, washed the cups with hot water, and brewed some tea. She called out "Dad" several times, but the old man kept his head down, showing no response.

Tongtong stretched out her chubby arms, which were like lotus roots, and timidly tugged at her grandfather's sleeve. Seeing no response, she lightly pinched her grandfather's arm with her fingers. This time, the old man's body shook violently. "What's wrong? What's wrong? Is there another problem at the oil field?"

"Dad, you've been retired for so many years, why do you keep remembering those things?" Xiao Ge handed over the tea again.

"Ret ... retired? How can I retire?"

Xiao Ge changed the topic. "Dad, have you had dinner? We're about to have our meal. Maybe there are not enough noodles, I'll go make some more."

"Noodles? Are they machine-made noodles or hand-rolled

noodles?"

"Just machine-made noodles."

"Is there any pulp?"

"No, we're out of liquorice pulp at home. Can you make do with it for now?"

"How can we make do with that?"

Meng Haiyun had never heard of liquorice pulp before. In order not to appear ignorant, she quickly searched on her phone—Oh, a kind of fermented vegetable juice for noodles. The webpage detailed the preparation steps, such as taking several types of vegetables, chopping them, adding yeast, stirring, and letting them ferment. Meng Haiyun looked at it, feeling a slight sourness on her tongue.

Xiao Ge didn't respond. She knew her father wasn't picky, he just had a stubborn attachment to traditional food. Xiao Ge tentatively said, "Dad, I'll go buy some liquorice pulp later. Let's just eat the noodles first, okay?"

Meng Qingshan shook his head and wasabout to say something, when he suddenly saw Meng Haiyun, scanning her up and down, and whispered to Xiao Ge, "Why did you bring your mum here too? She always nags me."

"What? My mum?" Xiao Ge was stunned, only then did she realise that her father mistook Meng Haiyun for her mother.

Meng Haiyun's features did indeed resemble her grandmother's when she was young, but her grandmother's appearance was already very vague in her mind. In Meng Haiyun's memory, taking care of her sick grandmother was one of the undeniable reasons why her father left Hainan to return to Dunhuang.

"No, no, this is your elder granddaughter, Haiyun."

"Nonsense, this is Haiyun." Meng Qingshan pointed at Tongtong, pulling her soft arm and lightly pinching it.

Xiao Ge was helpless, pointing at Meng Haiyun and Tongtong separately, saying word by word, "That, elder granddaughter, Haiyun. This, younger granddaughter, Tongtong."

Meng Qingshan nodded. "Got it. Haiyun, Tongtong, have you both eaten?"

"Dad," Xiao Ge reminded, "let's eat now, okay? The noodles are getting soggy."

"Oh, the noodles are getting soggy, then let's eat rice."

Just as Meng Haiyun was about to interject, she suddenly remembered the pot of rice that had gone mushy. She quickly jumped up and lifted the lid of the pot. The rice made a sizzling sound. Although the bottom was burnt, the top layer of grains remained crystal white, and the holes were evenly distributed. She quickly scooped out a bowl of rice, sniffed it under her nose: it was fine, with just a slightly strange smell, but still edible. She served it to her grandfather hurriedly.

Xiao Ge stir-fried a few vegetables to go with the noodles.

Meng Haiyun noticed that there was a lot of chili in it, so she cut a tomato, mixed it with sugar, and put it next to her. After everyone sat down, Tongtong picked up the sugar-coated tomatoes with her chopsticks first, followed by Meng Qingshan. Seeing that the dishes she prepared weren't too popular, Xiao Ge felt a bit disappointed. Since everyone liked the plate of tomatoes, she didn't touch it, just eating the dishes she herself made.

Meng Qingshan sat in Meng Peng's usual seat. Showing no interest in courtesy, he spread his arms like a protective bird, always using his wings to push aside the person next to him. Xiao Ge had no choice but to hold up her bowl to eat, but even so, her space was gradually shrinking. After a few bites, Meng Qingshan took off his slippers, pulled over a stool, and crossed his legs on it. But that was the stool where Tongtong placed her stuffed bunny. So the bunny had to sleep under the table, staring at everyone through its button eyes across the table. Tongtong wasn't happy about it, but Meng Qingshan was busy eating; with his eyes closed and legs crossed, he seemed to be enjoying his meal in meditation.

Tongtong couldn't eat without her bunny, so she took a few bites and then crawled under the table to look for it. Xiao Ge knocked on the bowl and said, "Come up, it's so dirty down there!"

Meng Qingshan looked at Xiao Ge. "Stop it, the child is

still young, being naughty is normal."

Xiao Ge had no choice but to give up. She picked up the sugar-coated tomatoes, thinking it wasn't right, but it wouldn't be appropriate to put them back, so she could only eat them. As a result, the dish Meng Haiyun made for herself became the first to be finished on the table. Meng Haiyun couldn't help but feel relieved.

After the meal, Meng Haiyun habitually cleaned up the dishes, but Meng Qingshan interrupted, "Haiyun has already cooked, don't let her wash the dishes."

Hearing this, Xiao Ge stacked the dishes together, making a clanging sound, and went into the kitchen. She made Grandpa misunderstand Xiao Ge, and Meng Haiyun actually felt quite guilty, so she couldn't help but look at Xiao Ge's back.

Meng Qingshan winked at the two children. "Haiyun, Tongtong, look what grandpa brought you."

He waved to the two children, then bowed his head and opened the woven bag at his feet. The zipper slid open to both sides, and the bag looked like it had been cut open from the middle.

Tongtong squatted beside him, eagerly staring at her grandfather's hands, which were rummaging through the bag like bird wings, pulling out things one by one. But each time, what came out wasn't what she wanted: a toothbrush, a slightly sour-smelling towel, a pair of dusty boots, a white safety helmet, a blue leather-covered notebook ...

Before long, the floor looked like a small grocery store. Tongtong saw her toys, usually thrown on the floor, buried underneath. She tried to pull out her toys from the pile of stuff her grandfather brought out, digging and digging until she finally grabbed the ear of her toy bunny. But then her grandfather said, "Found it!"

Tongtong immediately perked up like the ears of a rabbit, her hands placed expectantly on her chest, her eyes shining wetly, burning like coal, and her face beaming in the smoke. But when she saw what her grandfather held, the fire in her eyes extinguished all at once.

Meng Haiyun took a look, and felt disappointed to the core, just like her sister.

"A rock?"

That's it? Both Meng Haiyun and Tongtong felt disappointed and puzzled at the same time.

"This isn't a rock, it's an oil sand."

Indeed, it was a piece about the size of a palm, but its texture was different from ordinary rocks. Instead of being dense and hard, it was composed of layers of fine sand grains piled on top of each other, with a quite rough surface. When touched, the sand fell off like raindrops. Upon closer inspection, there were even some white salt crystals inside.

"Smell it, give it a sniff."

Meng Qingshan brought the oil sand close to Tongtong's nose. She immediately recoiled as if startled, wrinkling her nose and saying, "What's that smell?"

"It's the smell of oil, the smell of petroleum!"

Curious, Haiyun leaned in to smell. The smell of the oil sand seemed to grow hands, grabbing her, rolling around in her nostrils, forming a film wherever it went, quickly expanding its territory and invading her brain. It was a colourful odor, with black mixed with mottled green and white; it was layers of plant and animal remains accumulated over years, flowing in the bosom of the earth.

"Is this oil?" She closed her eyes, her whole body seemingly floating in the heavy smell of oil.

"This oil sand can catch fire."

"Really? Rocks can burn?"

"Do you know how the oil fields in Qinghai were discovered? It was because someone accidentally found that a kind of black rock could catch fire, which provided a clue to the exploration team. Later, a large area of oil sand mountains with these rocks was discovered, and then came the big oil fields."

"What happened next? Grandpa, tell us more." Meng Haiyun leaned in closer, not sure why, but she loved hearing about the past like this.

"We'll talk about it later, what's the rush? Let me give you the gifts first."

"Do I have a gift too?"

This time, the old man didn't put in much effort, just pulling out a small porcelain jar. When the jar was opened, there was a tiny seashell inside. How small was it? About the size of Meng Haiyun's pinky nail. She put it on her nail, examining its extremely faint lines. Being born by the seaside, she had seen many seashells, some big and brightly coloured. For such a plain shell, she didn't find it particularly special.

It seemed like Meng Qingshan noticed something and said, "This is a shell from the Qaidam Basin."

"Huh? How could there be seashells in the Qaidam Basin?"

"There really are! There's a place called Seashell Ridge there, which is a small ridge several kilometres long built up of shells of all sizes. On top is a thin layer of saline-alkali soil, and underneath are all these shells. I thought, you might have seen plenty of shells by the seaside, but shells in the desert, you probably haven't seen before."

"Oh." Meng Haiyun stopped playing with the shell, holding it in her palm and looking at it seriously.

"Did there used to be a sea in the place called Seashell Ridge?" Meng Haiyun asked.

"This question has been asked before, and I specially noted down the answer."

Grandpa picked up the blue leather notebook, its corners worn out, with two words printed on it: Work Notes.

Opening the notebook, there were yellowed pages, the corners had become hard and stuck together, like packaging paper. He carefully separated the fragile and wrinkled pages, flattening the stuck corners, and after searching a while page by page, he cleared his throat and began to read: "Geologists have found that in ancient times, the Qaidam Basin was a sea. Later, the sea turned into a lake, and the lake's water level dropped year by year, eventually drying up and revealing the lakebed. As for the shellfish, in order to survive, they all swarmed to the central water pit, and eventually accumulated more and more. But later, they still lost to geological changes. Instead of diminishing, the wind and sand became more severe, and eventually, the shellfish here became extinct."

Meng Haiyun couldn't help but stare at the notebook, feeling a strong desire to see what else was written inside. She really wanted to understand her grandfather more. She knew that her father's return to Qinghai and their family's change in trajectory were closely related to her grandfather. It was her grandfather who had altered the course of their entire family's life. She still remembered when she was young, she had visited their ancestral home in Tianshui, and her grandparents often came to stay shortly with them in Hainan. Whenever she misbehaved and her parents wanted to scold her, her grandfather always came out to mediate. Usually, he could always find reasons for her to avoid punishment, such as saying that children should be curious, they should play more, it's good that they have courage,"You weren't even as good as her when you were little," and so on, leaving her parents speechless. Later, no matter what happened in the family, her grandfather would often call to ask about her life and studies, and their home would frequently receive things he sent, sometimes food, sometimes clothes. Her mother would politely accept and thank him, but she didn't allow Meng Haiyun to touch those things. The food her mother would give away, the clothes would be folded and put away, hidden away until Meng Haiyun couldn't fit into them anymore ... She had always been like this, caught between her mother's emotions and her grandfather's love, being very careful. Blood-related affection didn't need to be shouted about or reminded day and night; it flowed in her veins. However, her mother's passing was like sand being poured into the vein of affection, rubbing her raw and making her feelings towards her grandfather also become complicated. If it wasn't for her grandfather, her father wouldn't have had to leave Hainan. If her father hadn't left, their home in Hainan would still be there, and her mother wouldn't have left—this impossible hypothetical scenario was like an invisible wall standing in front of her, yes, she had bound herself, but she wanted to break through that wall.

"Grandpa, do you have more interesting tidbits like those in your notebook? I really like them. Can you show it to me?"

"Hah, what's there to see? Besides, you might not understand my handwriting."

As if to prove his point, he casually flipped open a page and showed Meng Haiyun the handwriting on it. Grandpa's handwriting wasn't hard to recognize. Although it was cursive, the strokes were clear and strong, even clearer than some teachers' board writing. However, the words on it, written in blue ink pen, had faded somewhat.

Meng Haiyun smiled and said, "There's nothing I can't recognise. This says:

'I'd rather live twenty years less, but I will strive to conquer the big oil field!'

And this one:

'Where there's oil, there's home ... '

"Grandpa, were these slogans from your time?"

"Back then, it was like this, everyone was impassioned."

"Do you remember anything else interesting?"

Grandpa handed her the notebook and said, "You can look for yourself."

As he handed over the notebook halfway, a stack of folded paper fell out with a flutter. Before Meng Haiyun could see clearly, Grandpa bent down to pick it up and stuffed it into his pocket.

Meng Haiyun wanted to ask what that was, but then she worried it might be something Grandpa didn't want others to see. She felt too embarrassed to ask, so she took the notebook, carefully flicking through the yellowed pages, searching between the ink-splattered words—

There are no birds in the sky, no grass grows everywhere.

Little rain and snow in all four seasons, the wind blows the stones away.

Under the scorching sun, on top of hot sand.

Cold winds blow in winter, mosquitoes bite in summer.

Lacking drinking water for a whole month, never taking a bath all year.

Fingernails used as soup spoons, sand used to fry lice ...

Before she could finish reading, Meng Qingshan immediately burst into laughter and continued, "But as long as there's oil and gas, everyone says it's good!"

"This was written by our 'scholar' in the team," Meng Qingshan's face blushed slightly, and a glimmer of light shone in his cloudy eyes. "That year, we confirmed the thickness of the oil sand layer and discovered several oil seeps. We could work in the Qaidam Basin for a lifetime, and still wouldn't be able to extract all the oil!"

Xiao Ge had finished tidying up the dishes by now, shaking off the water droplets from her hands as she walked out. She reminded everyone that it was getting late, and Grandpa had been busy on the road all day, so he should sleep early, and the bedding needed to be adjusted. Seeing this, Meng Haiyun had to close the notebook and hand it back to Grandpa, and she volunteered to sleep on the sofa. So Xiao Ge and her daughter slept on the bunk bed, while Meng Qingshan slept on the double bed in the master bedroom.

In the middle of the night, a wave of overwhelming hunger struck Meng Haiyun, almost waking her up immediately. She missed meat buns so much, those big meat buns that oozed oil with just one bite. How could she not be hungry? She didn't cook much rice, and even ruined some of it, so she tried to eat less. But could her stomach be fooled so easily?

She sneaked into the kitchen, quietly turned on the stove, and prepared to cook herself a bowl of noodles in the dark. There were instant noodles in the cupboard, so she lit the stove, poured water, and put the noodles in, even the blue flames were silent—how ceremonial it all felt. She scooped up a chopstick and sniffed it, and it smelled so good! But as soon as the noodles touched her tongue, the kitchen door was opened.

The light snapped on, and Meng Haiyun saw a narrow band of light pouring from the crack of the kitchen door straight to her feet. She was scared and hurriedly threw the noodles back into the bowl. The next moment, a large head squeezed through the narrow crack of the door, with fluffy hair brushing against the door frame, and with a push, the whole person appeared in the kitchen.

"Grandpa?"

Meng Qingshan was wearing pyjamas; the fabric was soft and slack, swaying around him. He came to the refrigerator, muttering softly.

"Grandpa, what are you talking about?"

He opened the refrigerator door, rummaged under a pile of vegetables, grabbed two eggs, and handed them to Meng Haiyun. "Look, these are the food the refrigerator has given us."

Meng Haiyun laughed. If she were a few years younger, she would probably believe it. Now, she watched as Grandpa cracked the eggs on the edge of the pan with two taps, the egg white and yolk flowed into the pan like saliva, turning into poached eggs.

Meng Haiyun was about to eat when Meng Qingshan grabbed her wrist and stared at her, asking, "Old lady, how come your hair is still black when I'm aging like this? And where are your wrinkles?"

Here we go again, another case of mistaken identity.

Meng Haiyun had to explain again, "No, no, I'm your granddaughter, your elder granddaughter, Hai—Yun—"

"Isn't Haiyun sleeping inside?" Meng Qingshan pointed to the bedroom.

Meng Haiyun thought, why can't he understand? She sighed inwardly and when she looked up again, another person stood in the narrow beam of light from the kitchen door. This time it was Xiao Ge.

Meng Haiyun was startled, the bowl flipped, and the egg fell to the ground. Xiao Ge was also taken aback. "Why are you not sleeping and coming to the kitchen in the middle of the night?"

"I'm not full," Meng Qingshan hurriedly replied, patting Meng Haiyun's hand.

"Dad, you're getting old, you should sleep early," Xiao Ge said gently, and as she left, she closed the kitchen door, the light strip gradually disappearing.

"Oh, don't listen to her, I'm not old at all," Meng Qingshan slurped the noodles, shaking his head disapprovingly.

2

The first class in the afternoon was so drowsy.

The students who were as erect as newly planted saplings in the morning were now leaning all over the place, as if a typhoon had passed through. It's like as soon as the morning passed, something in their brains started chattering: "Tired, sleepy, so sleepy!" So the brain went on resting itself, leaving only an empty shell sitting in the classroom, staring at the teacher and the words on the blackboard.

But those words seemed to be like a flock of birds flying around; struggling to pin them down, the students reluctantly copied them into their notebooks. But if you looked closely, every word was restless, flying around, screaming, and clamoring to change places.

There were mistake after mistake on the notebooks, and yawns followed one after another from the students. If it weren't for the sudden noise outside of the window, there would have been even more people slumping.

Du Yiming casually glanced outside, and then couldn't take her eyes off. She rarely did this. Good students were the sunflowers of teachers, but today this sunflower's stem was bent, which made Ms. Huang very unhappy. If even the good students behaved this way, what was the point?

Ms. Huang raised his voice, trying to remind Du Yiming, but it was of no use. In just a short while, all the students were leaning and looking out of the window.

Ms. Huang put down her books and went to close the window, suddenly a "Yellow Dragon" came into view.

The Yellow Dragon wasn't a real yellow dragon; it was a group of camels. They were connected from head to tail, with a wooden stick horizontally across their noses, tied with ropes.

Camels were usually slow-moving animals. When they knelt down, they bent their knees on their front legs first, grunting as they touched the ground, then let their hind legs follow, and only then did they become solid; when they stood up, it was also slow, first straightening their front legs, then their hind legs with a thud, standing up. When camels walked, they were also slow, always looking like they were wandering in space, so they needed a guide. The camel guide led the camel, letting it move step by step, and walking and daydreaming at the same time.

Usually, camels were always leisurely, but the group of camels in front of them were running.

The leading camel seemed to have someone sitting in the middle of the hump, but the saddle was askew, so the person sitting on it was buffeted around, like he were drunk. He held

The Yellow Dragon wasn't a real yellow dragon;
it was a group of camels. They were connected
from head to tail, with a wooden stick
horizontally across their noses, tied with ropes.

onto the iron handle on the saddle tightly with both hands, lifting his butt every now and then to straighten himself up a bit. The huge backpack on his back also swung left and right with him.

The camels trotted on all fours, jumping, causing their double humps to sway up and down. Behind the camel team, there was also a car chasing after them, and the person in the driver's seat leaned out of the window, shouting at the camel team.

Many students heard the commotion and eagerly craned their necks to look.

This was somewhat bizarre. The camels in Dunhuang were usually concentrated in the Mingsha Mountain. Riding camels was a tourist attraction there, and it was rare to see them elsewhere. Mingsha Mountain was nearly ten kilometres away from Qili Town. Why did this old man lead these camels all the way to the school?

As soon as the camel team rushed into the campus, the principal and a group of teachers rushed over, blocking the camel team in front of the teaching building. At this time, the car that followed closely behind also stopped, and a person jumped out of the car, holding a whip, a neck loop from the neck to the head, and his face was completely covered by sunglasses and a straw hat. It was the typical outfit of the camel herders from Mingsha Mountain.

The principal had a square face and wore square black-framed glasses, with slightly thick lips. Such people generally had a bit of a stubborn temper but a good heart.

Everyone perked up their ears and listened attentively, and heard some intermittent conversations.

"Old dear, camels have owners, you can't just ride them whenever you want, and go wherever you want ..."

"That's not true! They didn't mistreat these camels! ... Did you make an appointment with someone to gather a camel team here? ... Who? Who did you make an appointment with?"

"Old dear, this is a school! ... When did it become a school? Ah, it's been more than ten years! ... Yeah, so you must be mistaken."

"Who do you say I look like? ... I don't know that person, and besides, how I look like someone has nothing to do with this. The key is that you're disrupting the students' class ..."

The old man's mouth trembled, his thin nose twitched, looking on the verge of tears. "I can't lead these camels away? Then what do we do? There are only a dozen or so, still a long way from the 350 camels we need to gather. These camels need to carry a lot of things—food, water, tents, pots, and tools for exploration. How can we just let people ride them? Camels are lifesavers, we need to get into the basin!"

"Basin? Are you talking about the Qaidam Basin?" The principal seemed to catch a clue, "Are you mistaken? The basin has already been explored."

"How can you speak like this? How is it me who's mistaken?"

The principal felt as if he were punching cotton. "Old dear, where are your family members? Let them come and take you home, alright?"

The camel driver with sunglasses interjected, "Go back? Hold on, let's settle the accounts first. Renting so many camels costs quite a bit ..."

The old man panicked at the mention of money, hastily waving his hand. "Money? How can money be involved? We're exploring oil for the motherland, how can we talk about money? Besides, we all agreed to meet here, where are the others? Where did everyone go?"

Students by the window were all looking out, and Meng Haiyun hadn't intended to join in the commotion, but the restless glances from her classmates annoyed her, prompting her to glance out of the window. That glance propelled her out like a cannonball. Even Ms. Huang couldn't stop her, only asking from behind: "Where are you going?"

"That's my grandfather!"

"Who?"

"The one riding the camel, my grand—pa—" Meng Haiyun was already out, her voice trailing behind her like a comet, taking a while to land in everyone's ears.

The classroom erupted once again.

The camels had already laid down in the schoolyard, twisting around and scratching themselves. A girl dashed out of the classroom, heading straight for the old man weeping by the camel. After talking with the her for a bit, the principal let her go over.

"Look, my old lady came to see me off." The old man proudly looked at Meng Haiyun, telling the principal, "Everyone else may forget, but she would never forget about me."

"She's your granddaughter," the principal said.

"Then, where is my wife?" The old man searched helplessly around, circling round and round, "I want to see her, I want her to see me off ..."

His wrinkles began to gather, his features seemed to converge towards the centre. Then, rain started to fall on this arid face.

Meng Haiyun hugged her grandfather tightly, comforting him like a child. The onlookers fell silent, realizing that the old man needed to go to the hospital. The camel driver grumbled about which family couldn't take care of their senile old man and began to lead the camels away, heading out of the school gates.

"Um, this student, you should go home for today and take care of your grandpa ..." After some thought, the principal added, "Your grandfather may be having memory issues, it's best to take him to the hospital for a check-up."

Meng Haiyun's heart tightened, suddenly recalling the incidents at home where her grandfather mistook her identity. She had thought it was just muddle-headedness due to old age, but now it seemed the problem might be more serious.

The bell for the end of class rang, and this class was a mess. Ms. Huang sighed as she tidied her books, and the students dispersed, some running straight to the school gate to join the crowd.

Meng Haiyun hadn't come back to herself yet until her clothes were gently tugged. Turning around, she saw Du Yiming and Yu Junying.

Du Yiming asked with concern, "What happened?"

Meng Haiyun snapped out of her daze, "I need to take my grandfather to the hospital for a check-up. He was fine yesterday, telling me stories about discovering oil. How come today his mind seems a bit unclear?"

"To the hospital? Do you have enough money?" Du Yiming asked, not waiting for an answer before turning to Yu Junying, "Can you lend some money to Haiyun?"

"Sure, but remember to pay me back!" Yu Junying quickly transferred money to Meng Haiyun's WeChat account.

Meng Haiyun looked gratefully at the two, "Thank you, Ming, Ying!"

"Bah, stop with the Ming and Ying, it's gross! Remember to

pay me back!"

Du Yiming patted Meng Haiyun's shoulder reassuringly, "Don't worry, no matter what happens, we're here for you."

The figures of three girls and an old man were reflected in the eyes of the camels. Their eyes bulged outward, like convex mirrors, distorting everything into curves. For the camels, there was no need to understand everything, just silently watching was enough.

For thousands of years, camels had seen too much. They didn't speak, just lifted their front legs, then their hind legs, shook off the sand, chewed on dry grass in their mouths, and slowly walked away.

The school returned to its calm state. The sunlight bathed the earth and the camels, casting undulating shadows on the classroom windows.

3

Meng Haiyun and Meng Qingshan walked out of the school gate.

The world was too strange! Every day, she looked forward to getting through school quickly, but one day, when she didn't have to go to school, she didn't know where to go while walking on the main road.

Meng Qingshan leaned against Meng Haiyun, suddenly turning into a child. Whom to find? Meng Haiyun quickly screened through the people she could turn to in her mind. Dad was on a business trip, and distant water couldn't put out nearby fire. She didn't know where Xiao Ge worked. She wanted to take her grandfather to the hospital now, but ... Oh no, she forgot to ask where the hospital was.

How come she didn't know anything? Meng Haiyun became angry with herself.

Their immediate concern was resolved by a taxi driver. With a creak, the car stopped beside them, and the driver stuck out half his head, asking, "Where to?"

Grandfather remained silent throughout the journey,

clutching the car window with both hands, his hair rustling as it lifted and fell. Just as Meng Haiyun was hesitating how to bring up the topic of going to the hospital, she heard her grandfather shout, "Camels, camels!"

They saw a statue in front of a building by the roadside, depicting a group of people riding camels, gazing into the distance with lofty expressions.

Grandfather shouted again, "Get off, get off!"

Meng Haiyun had no choice but to take him out of the car. Above the building was written "Museum" in three characters. The two followed the crowd inside, where a guide came up to them. Meng Haiyun and the guide stared at each other, both stunned.

It turned out to be Xiao Ge. Xiao Ge was a museum guide? She was wearing a red uniform, with her permed hair completely down, unlike when she neatly tied it up at home. Seeing Meng Haiyun and Meng Qingshan, Xiao Ge's professional expression turned into a mixture of surprise and puzzlement.

"How did you find your way here?"

"We happened to pass by, and grandfather said he wanted to come in and take a look."

Seeing Xiao Ge relieved Meng Haiyun's worries, she quickly recounted what happened that afternoon. Xiao Ge furrowed her brows, sighed, and whispered, "Have you noticed signs of Alzheimer's disease in your grandfather?"

"What disease?"

It was the first time they spoke in such a tone.

"Alzheimer's disease, also known as senile dementia. Actually, he wasn't quite right when he was in Tianshui, his hometown. An old neighbour told your dad that he often grabbed others to talk about finding oil, saying it so often that everyone avoided him. I originally thought he was just getting old and talkative, but now, the situation seems more serious. On the first day he arrived home, he mistook you for your grandmother, do you remember? I looked it up, and face recognition loss is one of the symptoms. These days, I've been hesitating whether to wait for your dad to come back or take him to the hospital as soon as possible."

The candid conversation made Meng Haiyun suddenly feel grown-up, like someone to discuss matters with.

"Getting treatment is the priority! Can Alzheimer's disease be cured with injections or medication? It doesn't matter if Dad isn't back, we can take care of grandfather together!"

Hearing them mentioning him, Meng Qingshan turned his head and asked, "Who are you talking about? Who has Alzheimer's disease? I, Meng Qingshan, have been working in oil exploration all my life. People who do oil exploration will never get Alzheimer's disease. I've memorised the geological epochs chart, that thing is really hard—should I recite it for you?"

Before getting a response, he raised a finger and began to talk animatedly: "During the Proterozoic era, fungi and primitive algae already existed, but there are few fossil records. In the late period, invertebrates appeared; next came the Paleozoic era, divided into the Cambrian, Ordovician, Silurian, Devonian, Carboniferous, and Permian periods; then came the Mesozoic era, with your favourite Jurassic period, when there were many dinosaurs and birds began to appear. But my favourite is the Cenozoic era, during the Quaternary period, the ancestors of humans appeared ..." The people around listened and applauded, some even shouted, "The old dear speaks well!"

Meng Haiyun almost wanted to take notes, so she wouldn't have to cram before the geography exam. As the old man got more excited, Xiao Ge, for once, didn't need to explain as a guide, smiling and encouraging him to continue. Suddenly, he changed the subject and asked Xiao Ge, "Do you know what kind of organisms produce oil and gas?"

Xiao Ge had only memorised the guide's script and was at a loss for words. The old man chuckled and somewhat smugly said, "Plankton, like blue-green algae and diatoms. You're a guide, and you don't even know this?"

Xiao Ge's face was full of helplessness. She seemed to want to save face in front of everyone, so she led them to a group of sculptures. She first introduced the old man riding a camel in the centre of the sculpture. His name was Yisha Aji, a Xinjiang guide for the basin exploration team at the time.

Without waiting for Xiao Ge to continue her introduction, Meng Qingshan immediately interjected, "This Yisha Aji is really useful!"

How was he useful? Grandfather enthusiastically recounted, and Meng Haiyun summarised it roughly—there were no roads in the Gobi, let alone fresh water. The land there was hardpan, salty, and alkaline, with salt seeping out of the surface, forming frost-like patterns under the sun. Digging for water with a shovel, all they got was sand, more sand with each shovelful. After digging all day, they finally found a handful of fresh water, but it tasted bitter. Finally, this guide was recruited. He led the exploration team travelling acrossone Gobi desert after another, crossing one salt marsh after another. He knew every fresh water source and understood the growth patterns of every kind of fauna and flora on the Qinghai-Tibet Plateau.

"Grandpa, I remember you were a soldier before, when did you go for exploration?"

"I joined the army when I was in my teens. In 1956, the country gradually organised soldiers to participate in oil field construction, and I went to the Qaidam Basin. That was the third year of exploring the Qaidam Basin. The days were tough ... you know? Just riding camels, trekking with Aji like this ..." Meng Qingshan continued, his steps lively, "It's said that the government wanted to specially grant him a car, but he refused to ride in it. While others despised camels, he, on the contrary, despised cars!"

Hearing her grandfather recalling the days so clearly, Meng Haiyun couldn't connect him with senile dementia.

In front of the sculpture, there was a large sand table of the Qaidam Basin. Xiao Ge pointed to several places on the sand table with her pointer, saying, "This is the Qinghai oil field, and to the west is the Huatugou production base, surrounded by the Kunlun Mountains, Altyn-Tagh, and Qilian Mountains."

"Which part is the Kunlun Mountains?" Meng Qingshan stared at the sand table and asked.

"Here," Xiao Ge pointed to a mountain range, and the snow line on the model undulated with the contours of the mountains.

"Look, there is snow on the Kunlun Mountains. Back then, Peng Peng was laughed at by his wife, who said there couldn't be snow in August. See? There's snow."

Peng Peng was Dad's nickname, and Grandpa was talking about Mum and Dad's affairs. Perhaps Xiao Ge felt uncomfortable? Meng Haiyun stole a glance at Xiao Ge, but there was no change in her expression, and she continued with her explanation. There were many winding lines on the sand table, and she pointed with a swoosh of her stick, saying, "This is our oil pipeline—after the oil is extracted from the ground, it has to be transported through special pipelines ..."

"Hexi Corridor! No, this should be the Hexi Corridor!" Meng Qingshan interrupted her again.

Xiao Ge took a look, and sure enough, she had pointed the oil pipeline to the position of the Hexi Corridor. She quickly moved her stick back.

Xiao Ge was about to continue his explanation when Meng Qingshan shouted again, "I'll test you. Which was China's earliest oil field?"

Before Xiao Ge could speak, Meng Qingshan gave out the answer: "Yumen Oilfield!"

Xiao Ge continued explaining how to determine the oil content by slicing oil-bearing rocks. Those slices of rocks, clustered with coloured grains, some indigo mixed with brown dots, and some brown mixed with gold flakes, didn't look like rock slices at all but more like marble from a construction materials market.

"How can you tell there's oil from this? How can you tell how much oil there is?" Meng Haiyun browsed through the slices, wondering where the black oil was hidden.

"One way is to look at the degree of impregnation, and the other is the porosity. The higher the impregnation of the rock, the higher the oil content; the larger the porosity, the more oil there is." Meng Qingshan answered eagerly.

Xiao Ge knew that the old man was in high spirits because of the crowd: he got excited and wanted to show off. She smiled and said, "Explaining is my job as a guide, let me finish first. If there's anything inaccurate, please help me correct it, okay?"

Meng Qingshan reluctantly agreed but added, "If you don't know, just ask. I know everything." Then, he stared at Xiao Ge with an extremely eager and focused gaze. Xiao Ge was usually a fast-talker, with words pouring out like popping beans, but under his gaze, even the well-prepared words got stuck.

There were many photos of oil field production bases in the exhibition hall, all set against barren landscapes.

Meng Haiyun sighed, "It looks so desolate!" Meng Qingshan said, "That's how it is there." Suddenly, he bent over, clutching his stomach, his face showing a painful expression. Upon asking, it turned out he needed to use the restroom. Meng Haiyun pointed in the direction of the restroom, but no matter what she said, he refused to go. After finally figuring out why he refused to go, it was both funny and exasperating: he was afraid to go—"Both camel urine and my urine must be kept to stay alive!" She turned on the tap, reassuring him that there was no shortage of water now, before coaxing him inside.

After coming out of the restroom, they continued their tour. Passing through a corridor, Meng Qingshan suddenly stopped in front of a black and white photo on the wall.

It was the Martyr's Memorial Wall. The photo in front of Meng Qingshan was of a person named Xiao Chanzhi, accompanied by a brief introduction of his life. Xiao Chanzhi was born in 1941, the same age as Meng Qingshan. In 1970, before he turned thirty, he lost his life in an accident while working for the oil industry.

"I was with him just a few days ago. Why is his black-and-white photo hanging here now? Take it down, take it down now ..." Meng Qingshan suddenly became anxious.

Meng Haiyun looked at her grandfather, who was staring anxiously at the photo, and suddenly realised that in her grandfather's memory, there was an amber, containing memories of a specific period of time. Sometimes he would confuse reality with the past, and if forcibly reminded of his mistake, he might be hurt.

Taking her grandfather home, Meng Haiyun felt for the first time that she was a guardian, guarding her fragile grandfather like guarding the last snowman of spring.

Meng Haiyun walked a few streets specifically to look for the so called "Jiangshui noodles"[1]. Someone told her that it was a snack beloved by people from Tianshui. Although Dunhuang was also in Gansu, not many people there ate it, so there was nowhere to buy it.

It seemed she would have to learn to make it herself, Meng Haiyun thought.

After taking a shower, Meng Haiyun changed into her

---

1   Known as jiangshuimian in Chinese, sometimes translated as sourherb noodles, also called sour water noodles, which are made by fermenting vegetables.

pyjamas and started writing in her diary. Suddenly, she heard the sound of a brush vigorously scrubbing tiles in the bathroom. She rushed in and saw Xiao Ge scrubbing the toilet vigorously, the brush swiping across the tiles like a wire ball.

There was some sticky residue on the floor of the toilet, and a few strands of soft long hair. Meng Haiyun had always been very careful about personal hygiene. For example, her clothes never occupied the drawers in the house; instead, she bought a separate basket to put them in a corner. After taking a bath, she would carefully pick out her fallen hair. Her dirty clothes were never mixed with others' for washing; they were piled up and washed clean at once. No one asked her to do this, Xiao Ge treated her well, never asked her to do housework, and never got angry with her. But that kind of politeness proved that there was still some distance between them. She wanted to avoid causing any trouble to this family; she was afraid her father would be embarrassed, and even more afraid that this hard-to-find place of refuge would leave her again.

Xiao Ge was vigorously scrubbing the tiles, and Meng Haiyun blushed at the sight. Although she had already tidied her hair, there was still a big lump stuck in the drain.

"Auntie, let me do it."

"No need, no need, you go and do your things."

Meng Haiyun and Xiao Ge were wrestling over the floor brush, when suddenly, there was a loud bang from the kitchen, followed by a sharp cry from Tongtong. Without thinking, Xiao Ge pushed away Meng Haiyun, who was blocking the door, and rushed into the kitchen.

It turned out that the thermos broke, and Tongtong's feet were scalded by the splashing water. Meng Haiyun felt extremely guilty when she saw this. In fact, the thermos was not originally placed in such an exposed location. It was she who didn't put it back to its original place after pouring water, which led to Tongtong getting hurt. Xiao Ge picked up Tongtong, quickly treated her wound, and then rushed out. Meng Haiyun followed closely behind, her pyjamas lifting up, revealing her bare legs. The slippers made a hollow echo as they hit the floor in the corridor.

Xiao Ge carried Tongtong into the car, and Meng Haiyun asked if she could go with them. Xiao Ge just said, "Help me take care of grandpa at home," then drove off.

The window at the end of the corridor reflected the sky, dark and sticky like dripping oil. Someone had lit it up, and the dotting fire was the lights.

Without darkness, there is no light. Light floats, connecting dots into surfaces, rippling in the city. Darkness descends calmly, bearing the unseen wind and sand. Everyone has a mountain in his heart, throwing that mountain into the shadow is like throwing ice into the Mariana Trench, it disappears instantly.

The temperature difference between morning and evening

084

in Dunhuang is significant. Meng Haiyun was only wearing pyjamas and was shivering with cold. The last time she stood in the corridor wearing pyjamas like this, she had quarreled with her mother and had run out of the house in a fit of anger.

She knew her mother would chase after her quickly. She somewhat sweetly listened to the chaotic noise of shoes in the shoe cabinet at the door, followed by the clinking of keys and the hurried footsteps on the stairs. Her mother embraced her and scolded, "You left because of a few scolding words? Running out in so little clothing, what if you catch a cold?"

If her mother was a thread, she was a needle. Only by threading the needle could the warmth of the home be woven. Without the thread, she would become a needle that could only prick herself.

"Mum, mum ... where are you ..." Meng Haiyun stretched out her fingers, trying to grab the imaginary face of her mother. But her vision gradually blurred, and the face disappeared into the darkness.

She couldn't help but take out her phone, wanting to call her grandmother on her mother's side, but before her grandmother could answer, she hung up. It was late, her grandmother should be asleep, and a phone call wouldn't help; it would only worry her grandmother unnecessarily.

"Come back if you can't stand it", her grandmother always said that. Her grandmother's house was her last resort.

A last resort is a path that must not be taken unless absolutely necessary.

She had to go home. Even if Xiao Ge hadn't left that sentence asking her to take care of her grandfather, she couldn't escape back to Hainan. Meng Haiyun slowly walked home, and to her surprise, the door was wide open. Grandpa was pacing at the door, eagerly looking outside. As soon as he saw her, he ran over and grabbed her arm, pulling her into the house, and the door slammed shut behind them.

"Where did you go? Where did you go? I was so worried ..."

Meng Haiyun's heart, which had been like a fish out of water, began to swim happily again. Someone was waiting for her, someone had always been waiting for her.

Meng Haiyun said softly, "It's okay, Tongtong ..."

Grandpa stared, "It's okay? Did you lose the camels again? Let's see how you'll carry luggage tomorrow!"

"What luggage?"

"What luggage? Water, dry food, pots. Find a bigger bag with two straps, a backpack." Grandpa went to pick up his backpack, the one he had been swinging on his back when he rode the camel into the school. He unzipped it with a swish, revealing a bunch of miscellaneous items such as compressed biscuits, military water bottles, spatulas, etc.

"See? You need to prepare these. You don't have this kind of bag, do you? I'll lend you mine." He emptied the bag with a swish and handed the empty bag to Meng Haiyun. "Take it, remember to pack your things tomorrow morning, got it?"

Meng Haiyun could only nod continuously as she looked at the pile of stuff on the ground and the gaping bag.

The next morning, when she woke up, Grandpa was already in the living room fully armed, waiting for her.

She had a hard time making Grandpa understand that she was going to school, not for exploration. She was Meng Haiyun, not her grandmother. The old man walked back to the house, half-believing and half-doubting.

At school, Meng Haiyun blurted out all the family affairs to Du Yiming as soon as she saw her. She felt relieved after spelling it out, as if a burden had been lifted from her heart. But Du Yiming was Du Yiming, she always had her own ways. As soon as school was over, she dragged Meng Haiyun home to find her senior advisor—her mum.

Du Yiming's mother was named Wang Hui. She had been a journalist for more than ten years, decisive in her actions and eloquent. Du Yiming had already told her mother about Meng Qingshan's illness, so as soon as they entered, Wang Hui pulled Meng Haiyun to sit down.

Wang Hui said to Meng Haiyun, "There are indeed experts in Dunhuang in this field. I've interviewed an old man before whose situation was very similar to your grandfather's. I consulted a doctor specifically on how to treat it. The doctor said that the cause of this disease is unknown. Your grandfather's generation of oil workers had suffered a lot in their early years. Even if their physical fitness was good, it was inevitable to leave behind some hidden health issues. These might all be causes. There's also another situation where a certain period of time is very important and unforgettable for the elderly, but there's a knot in their heart that they can't untie, so their memory always gets stuck in that specific period of time. For people with this disease, time is chaotic, and the faces of people in their minds are also chaotic. As the disease progresses gradually, they may experience language confusion, memory loss, forgetting the names of everyday items, and so on. In the later stages, they need someone to take care of them all the time. I speculate that your grandfather may have realised his condition and wanted to revisit the oil field before completely losing his normal living ability. Perhaps he won't have the chance in the future. If forcibly stopped, he might get anxious, which willworsen his condition, so it's better to defer to him."

"Defer to him? He wants to go back to the Qaidam Basin for exploration. Should we defer to him?"

"Of course, we should defer to him with a purpose. Nobody knows what his knot exactly is, and the doctor also believes that if we can help the elderly return to past circumstances, untie their knots, and repeatedly emphasize and let them logically recall the names of people, things, and events, it may help slow down the progression of the disease."

"Earlier, when we went to the museum, Grandpa was extremely excited when he saw a martyr's name. Let me think ... Yes, the name was Xiao Chanzhi."

"Perhaps he was grandpa's former colleague. The clue you provided is very important. I need to think about it ..."

"And also, Auntie, my grandpa is almost eighty years old. If he goes back to the plateau, what if he gets altitude sickness?"

"I asked the doctor about this. Your grandpa has been working in the basin all his life, and his body has long adapted to it. There's no need to worry."

"But ... during the early exploration days, there was a shortage of food and supplies, not to mention that there were no roads in the desert. People had to ride camels ..."

"How about this, I'll go up there in a while and I can assist you. I can request a car, so instead of riding camels for a long journey, we can make the trip in a day or two by car. You can ask for a few days off from school."

"But what if Grandpa insists on riding a camel?" Meng Haiyun recalled the scene of her grandfather riding a camel to school at Mingsha Mountain.

"We can stage a play—find a specific location, let Grandpa ride a camel, recreate the scene for him, and we can play his past companions, accompanying him to revisit the old route, to see if it can help him retrieve those special memories."

"This ... seems quite complicated ..."

"I'll help you figure it out. But the key still lies with you. Do you want to help Grandpa resolve this inner conflict?"

"Of course. In Dunhuang, Grandpa is the closest person to me. As long as it's for Grandpa's good, I'm willing to do anything."

"Then taking a trip up there might even help alleviate your grandfather's condition—oh, 'up there' refers to Huatugou, you know?"

Du Yiming leaned over, whispering in her mother's ear, "Are you planning to go see my dad again? Do you want to take me with you?"

Her mother raised her voice, "Stop showing off! Let's see how you do on your mid-term exams this time. Let me tell you, if you fall out of the top three, forget about it."

"So, getting into the top three means I can go?" Du Yiming said, "That's simple."

Meng Haiyun looked at the mother and daughter, feeling a mix of envy and bitterness. She used to be the darling held in her mother's hands.

Du Yiming's mid-term exam results were indeed good, and her mother kept her promise, taking her along. They announced to others that they were going to see Du Yiming's father, Du Lang, and also take Meng Haiyun's grandfather to visit the places where he used to work.

Thus, the "Awakening Memories" special action team was established! Wang Hui was the team leader, and she had assigned tasks to each member. The team consisted of Meng Haiyun, Du Yiming, and Yu Junying, three girls, and a mysterious figure. Who the mysterious figure was, Wang Hui said, was to remain confidential for the time being.

Before departure, the three girls gathered at Du Yiming's house. Meng Haiyun and Du Yiming sat cross-legged on the sofa, while Yu Junying squatted on the floor packing luggage, occasionally putting some things in the suitcase, then tilting her head to check the suitcase, and occasionally asking Du Yiming if she needed to bring anything else, then running to get it and stuff it into the suitcase.

"She seems like your little maid," Meng Haiyun observed, tilting her head to look at Du Yiming.

"How dare you say that!" Yu Junying retorted irritably, "If it weren't for you, I would be resting by now."

At this moment, Du Yiming's mother walked over and said, "Oh, I knew someone would be chatting away, pushing all her work onto others!"

Upon hearing this, Du Yiming hurriedly pretended to put two pieces of clothing into the suitcase. As soon as her mother turned around, she let Yu Junying do it instead.

"Wow, our team is really strong!" Du Yiming secretly congratulated herself on her decision to bring Yu Junying.

A week ago, when they first discussed the trip at home, Du Yiming specifically told Meng Haiyun, "My mum is very tight-fisted when it comes to money. If you want to buy snacks or small items on the road, asking her won't work. But with Yu Junying, it's different, you know?"

"I know Yu Junying will have all kinds of snacks prepared in advance, but what if she doesn't share them with me? I can buy them with money."

"It's okay, I'll help you plead with her, and she might even give you a discount."

"You can get a discount on this too ..."

"That's settled then!" Du Yiming patted Meng Haiyun.

Yu Junying agreed as she expected. In fact, there was nothing she wouldn't agree to if Du Yiming asked. Du Yiming and Meng Haiyun stuffed the snacks they had at home into the suitcase, while Yu Junying angrily took out half of them and replaced them with thick clothes.

"There's a big temperature difference up there, you'll freeze to death without a down jacket, you know?"

"Oh, I see." Du Yiming answered.

After a while, Yu Junying ran back home again, bringing back a few sun hats. "The sun is scorching from 8 a.m. to 8 p.m. over there, you can't go without a hat, you know?"

"Oh, I see." Du Yiming replied again.

"All you ever say is 'I know'!"

"Then what else do you want me to say? It's good enough that you're worrying about these things." Du Yiming innocently stuck out her tongue.

With Yu Junying's concern, their luggage increased from the originally planned one suitcase to two, plus two carry-on bags. One of the carry-on bags contained hats, veils, sunglasses, windbreakers, while the other were filled with apples.

"Why do you take so many apples?" Meng Haiyun asked.

"They have high water content and can be kept for a long time, convenient to eat," Yu Junying said.

Meng Haiyun turned to Du Yiming and asked, "Do you like apples?"

"Yes, I love them. They're my favourite fruits."

See, that's the real answer. Yu Junying was indifferent to others, but when it came to taking care of Du Yiming, she was especially enthusiastic.

4

Meng Haiyun carefully packed her things, and most importantly, she had to choose a book to bring along. She used to have a habit that if there was something important to do the next day, she couldn't sleep at all the night before.

On sleepless nights, listening to others' breathing, she could only toss and turn, "counting sheep": the more she counted, the more awake she became; the more she counted, the more she looked forward to dawn. Later, when encountering such situations, she would read a book. Those books that she couldn't usually get into became particularly attractive in the quiet night. So, she decided to pick a book from her father's study.

She ran her fingers over rows of books on the bookshelf, pondering which one would be suitable for reading on a sleepless night. Finally, her finger stopped at *Eternal Monument* and she pulled it out, flipping through a few pages. She discovered that it was a chronicle of the Qinghai Oilfield.

The book recorded that in 1947, a group of scientists, including geologist Zhou Zongjun, went to survey the Qaidam Basin. They heard that someone was using a black stone to light a fire near a mountain in the western part of the basin. Following the clues, they finally discovered a thick layer of oil sandstone at a location. Everyone was surprised, and it was announced that there was oil in the Qaidam Basin from then on. After the founding of the People's Republic of China, the country sent geological teams into the Qaidam Basin for exploration, and since then, the Qinghai Oilfield has gradually been developed. The lives of several generations have been rewritten, grandfather, father, mother, and her ... Meng Haiyun secretly thought. It was as if an invisible hand had pushed her from the carefree life in Hainan to this land, this home mixed with the smell of oil sand.

Tongtong peeked into the study like a little cat. Meng Haiyun waved to her, "Tongtong, come in."

"Sis ... sis ..." Tongtong chirped and bounced over, "What are you doing?"

"Sister is reading a book."

"Oh, is it interesting?"

Tongtong came over, flipped through the book cover; though she hardly knew any characters, she pretended to read it and finally closed the book.

Meng Haiyun smiled. Tongtong had a littletrick of finding someone to play with her. Instead of directly asking, she would start a topic, making others be conscious of neglecting her, and then play with her. Just like now, she asked about the content of the book, but her body language showed that she didn't want Meng Haiyun to read.

This little girl already had a little bit of scheming.

"I'll play with you, what do you want to play?"

"Sister, are coconuts tasty?"

"Huh? Coconuts?"

Just mentioning the word "coconut" seemed to bring a sweet taste to her tongue. She suddenly realised that she hadn't eaten coconut for some time. In Dunhuang, apricots were produced, and the locals used apricots to make apricot skin water, a unique snack sold everywhere. Meng Haiyun liked to try new things, and she fell in love with it, but occasionally she would miss coconuts. Although the fruit shops in Dunhuang also sold coconuts, the price was high, and she wasn't willing to beg her father to buy them.

"Mum bought coconuts. She said you used to eat coconuts all the time, I also want to eat them. But Mum can't open the coconut shell, can you help her?"

It turned out she was only remembered when she was needed. Meng Haiyun's heart seemed to be soaked in apricot skin water, a bit sour and a bit astringent. Tongtong was looking at her expectantly, hoping she would quickly pry open the hard coconut shell. She really couldn't bear to let this little guy down.

No wonder there had been banging sounds coming from the kitchen since a while ago, loud enough to sound like someone was tearing the house down.

Meng Haiyun rushed into the kitchen and saw Xiao Ge applying all sorts of techniques to the coconut. She lifted the kitchen knife and chopped at the coconut, but the stubborn coconut only had a few white knife marks on its head. On the other hand, the countertop, which already had cracks, snapped a longer one with a "crack".

Xiao Ge looked up with a mournful face. "Why is this coconut so hard!"

"Sister, it's your turn," Tongtong tugged at Meng Haiyun.

"Uh, I don't know either ... In Hainan, coconut shells are already pre-drilled with holes, so you can just insert a straw and drink."

"Then both of you go over there, I'll handle this myself."

Meng Haiyun saw the light shining on Xiao Ge's woolly hair, and the frown on her face while drilling the coconut resembled her mother's. as long as she mentioned something she wanted to eat her mother would find a way to get it for her, or learn to make it herself. Her mother's figure was like a photo with frayed edges, swaying and fading on the surface of memory. Every child thinks their mother will always be by their side, forever and ever, never growing old, but looking back now, the time with her mother by her side was too short.

Meng Haiyun's memories came crashing in, burning fiercely, and when she came back to her senses, she saw that

Xiao Ge had already found the coconut's weak spot and had opened a few holes with a screwdriver. Since she hadn't found a bowl in advance to catch it, the coconut water dripped down her hand. When she frantically found a bowl, only a small amount of coconut water could be collected.

Tongtong couldn't wait and reached out for the bowl. Xiao Ge raised the bowl high over Tongtong's head and said, "There's too little coconut water, I'll give it to sister this time, Mum will buy it for you next time, okay?"

Although disappointed, Tongtong still nodded gently.

"Haiyun, I don't really know how to get along with a big kid like you, but since your dad isn't home, I hope to take good care of you. But now you're leaving again tomorrow. You've been in Dunhuang for so long, I guess you miss home. I'm not good at picking coconuts, I don't know if they're good, but it was really bought specifically for you."

Meng Haiyun took the bowl, feeling the smoothness of the porcelain with her fingertips and the warmth of Xiao Ge's fingers. She didn't move at all, but the melancholy slipped away quietly.

Tongtong extended a finger and asked, "Sis, can I just taste a little bit?"

Xiao Ge said, "Your hands are dirty, if you dip them in the bowl, how can your sister drink?"

But Tongtong had already quickly dipped her index finger

into the bowl and put it in her mouth. Xiao Ge looked at her sucking her finger and awkwardly smiled at Meng Haiyun, tentatively saying, "Her hands are not clean, so don't drink from the bowl." Then she scolded Tongtong, "Didn't I say I'll buy it for you next time?"

Meng Haiyun felt the sourness of apricot skin water in her heart again. What was she doing? Clearly, she was being sensitive and melodramatic, yet she let a preschooler give her something to eat.

She found a spoon and sat on the floor, holding Tongtong, sharing the little coconut water between them with a small spoonful each. The milky fragrance from Tongtong mixed with the aroma of coconut water. Meng Haiyun thought to herself, this little guy is her sister, and from today onwards, she had to act like a real sister.

After drinking, she looked up and winked at Xiao Ge.

5

The departure time was set at 8 a.m.

The car arrived; surprisingly, it was a small truck, and the driver wore sunglasses, covering most of his face. Even so, you could still see a ferocious scar on his cheek, flesh-pink, winding from the cheekbone to the corner of his mouth. This made his lips never fully closed, and half of his face seemed slightly askew.

Seeing him for the first time, the three girls were a bit nervous. The driver introduced himself as Mr. Yang and pointed enthusiastically at the thermos in the car, "There's water here, pour it yourself with a cup."

As he spoke, he placed the luggage one by one under the seats, tightly wedging them into the gaps. Clearly, there was still space at the back of the small truck, so they asked why he didn't put the luggage there. He smirked, "There are still big things to put there sa."

Local people like to add the word "sa" at the end of a sentence, they call it "word handle" Meng Haiyun found it quite cute, with a simple and honest charm.

What big things?

After a while, the "big thing" arrived—surprisingly, it was a small camel. How small? Its milky white fetal hair had just fallen off, and its light camel-coloured fluff was tightly attached to its body, with its thin legs trembling. The two humps were small and droopy, and one of them was even tilting to the side. It didn't look like a camel at all, but more like a big sheep.

"Put this into the car?" Everyone was stunned and kept saying, "Impossible, impossible."

"Why impossible?" Mr. Yang said, pushing the camel's butt towards the space at the back of the small truck. The poor little camel tried to raise its head, but its neck got stuck between the gaps of the two back seats in the end.

As the car door closed, the little camel knelt down and automatically adjusted its posture. It seemed that it could "flow" into any shape depending on the space given to it.

Mr. Yang patted the dust off himself with satisfaction, leaving the three girls dumbfounded. A live camel, squeezed into a sandwich, was really pitiful. It must be very uncomfortable.

Xiao Ge had already made several phone calls, asking if the car was ready. The old man was anxious to set out, and she could barely hold him back. Before Meng Haiyun could think of how to make the little camel more comfortable, she heard Meng Qingshan's anxious voice: "How can you go without me? Before the camel team sets off, we have to check the essential tools, supplies, dry food, and drinking water ... Oh my, if I don't check it, how can I feel at ease ..." Meng Qingshan walked out of the corridor of the apartment building, and as soon as he saw the small truck, he shouted anxiously, "Take the car? The car isn't even as good as the camel! Besides, the car runs on oil, and we're looking for oil. Driving to find oil, isn't that crazy?"

Xiao Ge followed closely behind, whispering to Du Yiming's mother, "Normally, I should also go you see, Haiyun is still a child, but I have an even younger one."

Du Yiming's mother hurriedly comforted her, "It's okay, it's okay, you relax, we have many people, and besides, they're all acquaintances up there."

Xiao Ge asked Meng Haiyun, "Have you got all your stuff? Nothing left behind?" Meng Haiyun quickly said yes, reassuring her. Xiao Ge wanted to say something more, but hearing Meng Qingshan's urgent shouting, she hurriedly helped him put the luggage into the car. When she opened the car door, she saw the little camel and couldn't help but exclaim, "Dad, look at the camel!"

Meng Qingshan, who had been refusing to get on the car, saw the little camel on the car, and his eyes suddenly froze. Those complaints, that stubbornness, the part of him that stiffened his neck and refused to accept modern things, crumbled away. He whispered and comforted the little camel while climbing into the back seat. Meng Haiyun saw Xiao Ge breathe a sigh of relief and pretended to say lightly, "With this little camel on the road, Grandpa won't be naughty." It sounded like she was talking to everyone, but also meant to reassure Xiao Ge. Xiao Ge took out a box of preserved plums from her pocket and said, "This is prepared by Tongtong for you. If you have slight altitude sickness, hold one in mouth to feel better. If it's too uncomfortable, don't force yourself, come down immediately."

Just as the car started moving, Xiao Ge suddenly tapped on the car window, and Meng Haiyun rolled down the window again. Xiao Ge reminded her, "Remember to call me if there's anything, and remember to call your dad every day."

"Oh, got it." Meng Haiyun quickly agreed. Xiao Ge reminded Mr. Yang to drive slowly for safty's sake on the road before letting them go.

"She's quite nice to you," Du Yiming said.

"You don't understand, that's just courtesy," Yu Junying said.

Just a few minutes after the car started, Meng Haiyun's phone rang, it was Xiao Ge. Did she forget to tell her something? But when she answered, it was Tongtong's childish voice calling out, "Sister, come back soon!"

It turned out Tongtong was too short to reach the car window and couldn't speak earlier, and she was so anxious to talk to Haiyun that she made Xiao Ge call immediately.

Meng Haiyun replied with "Okay okay okay," promising

to come back early to accompany her. As an only child, she genuinely liked this little sister, who made her feel needed. If she and Xiao Ge were the two pieces of bread of a hamburger, Tongtong would be the filling. Now she was willing to stick even closer to the other slice of bread.

The journey was calm, only the steady sound of the car driving. Originally, everyone was afraid the old man would have problems halfway through, but unexpectedly, he fell asleep in less than half an hour. His head was resting on the back of the seat, mouth slightly open, making a snoring sound.

Sometimes when the light was too strong, shining on his eyelids, he would grunt, briefly pausing his snoring. When you would think he was about to wake up, the snoring continued.

Meng Haiyun used her hand to block the flickering light and carefully studied her grandfather. Beneath his shiny forehead, was there a chaotic room? It seemed to be flooded, with tables and chairs floating around in disarray. His memory box was in disarray. He was trapped in that room and couldn't get out.

Was he thinking about the past again? He was furrowinghis brows, looking distressed; was he having a dream? What kind of dream made him so uneasy?

Mr. Yang glanced at the people in the rearview mirror. He often picked people up to go up there and was very familiar with who was related to whom in this town. He lowered his voice and asked Wang Hui, "The vacation hasn't started, right? So you're alreadying taking the child up to see her dad?"

Wang Hui said, "Bring a few more kids up this time, they've been eagerabout going up there."

Du Yiming interrupted, "It's so boring up there, who would be eager to go up there? It's because my dad sent me a red envelope of 200 yuan before by wechat, and I forgot to collect it. I have to get it back this time, I swear!"

"Oh, you're going through all this trouble for 200 yuan? Not many kids are willing to go up there.' Mr. Yang then asked Yu Junying, Little Yu, is your mum still on the plane?"

"Hmm." Yu Junying played with her phone, indifferent.

Mr. Yang knew her personality, so he stopped talking to her and glanced at Meng Haiyun through the rearview mirror, asking, "This child ... which family is she from?"

Meng Haiyun then introduced herself. The driver acknowledged, saying, "You're Engineer Meng's daughter from Hainan," then added, "You guys are a big gathering of 'oil kids'"

Only Meng Haiyun didn't understand what "oil kids" meant. It turned out that the offspring of those working in the oil fields were called "oil kids." If the grandfather worked in the oil fields, the son would also work there, then the son would be the "second-generation oil worker." Some families even had grandchildren working in the oil fields, then they would be the "third-generation oil worker."

Not willing to be always questioned, Meng Haiyun also had a lot of questions to ask: "Mr. Yang, why did you bring the camel into the car?"

"Someone up there wants to eat camel meat, but the big camel can't be brought over, so we brought the little camel."

"Eat? Isn't it too cruel to kill such a small camel? Besides, aren't camels very useful?"

"It's not like in the past, camels used to carry people and goods." Mr. Yang didn't think much of it. In his opinion, eating camel was no different from eating pork or chicken.

Meng Haiyun turned back to look at the little camel. It remained silent, kneeling on its legs, neck stretched out, its olive-shaped eyes blinking pitifully under long eyelashes—such a cute little guy, did it know it was about to be killed for its meat?

The scenery in its eyes flashed by with the swaying of the car. Had it seen the real desert and the Gobi? Would it look forward to walking the Silk Road tread by its ancestors with its little hooves? The camel had always silently endured the various arrangements of fate, helpless. But in the vast desert, travellers listened to the camel's breathing during long journeys, even if thirsty, they felt a sense of comfort in being alive.

Is it right to manipulate other creatures for the sake of humans? If she were this little camel, what would she be thinking at this moment?

"Maybe you think this is cruel, but it's a cycle of life, the law of nature." Wang Hui guessed Meng Haiyun's thoughts and said.

No one had ever told her these things before, Meng Haiyun listened very seriously, but still couldn't let go.

After going for over an hour, the car suddenly shook and stopped with a clatter. Meng Qingshan's body jolted, and his loud snoring abruptly stopped. He opened his eyelids: "Are we here?"

"Old dear, we haven't arrived yet, do you want to sleep a little longer?" Mr. Yang pulled out a blanket and helped him covered up.

At some point, the car had stopped amidst the snowy mountains. The scenery before along the road had been typical urban scenes, but after a nap, they had broken into the domain of the towering snow-capped peaks.

"What mountain is this?" Meng Haiyun asked.

"It's the Dangjin Mountain," Mr. Yang replied.

Meng Haiyun remembered seeing it on the sand table before, along with the Qilian Mountains and the Kunlun Mountains, all vast mountain ranges, rugged and desolate. When Zhang Qian went on his mission to the Western Regions, it must have been quite difficult ...

"What? We're at the Dangjin Mountain? That doesn't seem right, we got here too quickly ..." Meng Qingshan couldn't sit still; he opened the car window and looked out. The snowy mountains stood abruptly in front of them, like an opening mouth, and cold wind gushed out from between their teeth, rushing into the cramped space of the car. Everyone hugged their arms and shrank into their seats.

"Where are the camels?" Meng Qingshan lifted the blanket and was about to get off.

Mr. Yang quickly pointed to the little camel behind, "The camels, the camels are here."

Du Yiming was closest to the camel, and she patted its head and urged it to move closer to grandpa. The little camel was on it kneesand tried hard to lift its butt to stand up. Meng Qingshan's attention was immediately drawn to the little camel, who looked pitifully at the old man.

Between high cliffs, twisting slopes and winding roads stretched between the mountains, with many cars connected end to end, struggling to move forward on the narrow road between the mountains.

"Why did we stop?"

Mr. Yang looked ahead, "There may have been an accident. Accidents are common on this road. When it snows, it turns into an icy mess, melting during the day and freezing at night. The most dangerous are those big trucks. Once they slip and flip over ... oh, that's a disaster!"

It was Meng Haiyun's first time seeing a snowy mountain,

and she couldn't help but roll down the car window.

Snow was the soul of these mountains, lightly sketching the texture and veins of the mountains between the mountain peaks. Along the borderline between light and shadow, the snow traces crisscrossed, resembling the veins of leaves from a distance, and also like a string of shiny hair bands on a girl's head; the scenery was extremely beautiful. Without snow, the mountains would just be huge lumps of dirt.

Upon closer observation, the amount of snow on the mountaintops on both sides of the road was different, obviously more on one side than the other. The side with less snow looked like it had been shaved bald. Meng Haiyun voiced her doubts.

"This side is sunny, the other side is shaded." Mr. Yang pointed to both sides of the mountain, "The shaded side has more snow and looks better. Haven't you seen a snowy mountain before? Go down and take a look. Besides, you need to adapt. When we get up there, the altitude is two to three thousand metres, you won't be able to handle it all at once. Let's make some adaptation here first."

Meng Haiyun jumped out of the car, followed by Du Yiming and Yu Junying. Wang Hui hurriedly shouted, "Hey, I didn't ask you two to get off, what's the rush?"

Du Yiming turned around and teased, "Go— to— the— toi— let—"

The air was cold and crisp, as if it had just been frozen

in the refrigerator and slapped onto her face with a snap. Meng Haiyun shivered a few times, didn't feel any discomfort, and focused on observing the surrounding environment: the road was covered with a thin layer of snow, some stubborn camel thorns protruded from the frozen soil; hoof prints of quadrupeds were faintly lined up, lonely imprints on the snow, coming from nowhere and going nowhere.

"Those are left by the grazing cattles of herdsmen." Du Yiming drew a range of mountains along the footprints, "You see, the cattle and sheep have to cross the Dangjin Mountain like this to reach the Alar Grassland."

Really? Are there still people grazing now?

Meng Haiyun saw her own footprints intersecting with theirs by chance. Crossing the snowy mountains on foot was something she couldn't imagine. Although they lived in the same world, their lives were very different. But there was one thing in common—they were both lonely and free here.

Du Yiming and Yu Junying said they were going to find a restroom, but actually, they wanted to secretly discuss how to rescue the little camel.

The two girls stood in front of a roadside map sign. To provide convenience for tourists, the map marked every nearby scenic spot in detail. Meng Haiyun approached curiously, only to hear them muttering, "There are camels raised by herdsmen in the pasture next to the highway. If we release the little camel there, it should be able to survive, right?"

"But how can we get it off the car?" Du Yiming frowned.

"Did you forget about someone?" Meng Haiyun bounced over, pointing to herself.

The two girls were startled, and when they came back to their senses, they hurriedly explained that they were afraid Meng Haiyun wouldn't agree to let the camel go because they could see that her grandfather had stabilised emotionally after seeing the camel, so they discussed it secretly.

"You guys underestimate me too much. I want to protect my grandfather, but I also want to protect the camel! Where did you guys stop at just now? Actually, I got an idea ..." Meng Haiyun stepped forward, and the three girls huddled together to discuss ...

After a while, the car convoy started to moveslowly. The snowy mountains glared fiercely, as if they would forever detain the cars if they dissented, so each car proceeded cautiously.

After the snowy mountains, there was the Gobi Desert. It stretched endlessly, dry, hard, and vast, as if a giant hand had smeared mud on the earth and let it dry and harden. Upon closer inspection, a layer of white frost could be seen on top. Wang Hui said it was salt, seeped from underground, and such places were called saline-alkali land, where except for camel thorns, other plants could barely survive. "The salt here could meet the need of several generations for the whole nation, there's so much of it," said Mr. Yang.

"So salt actually grows like this from the ground!" Meng Haiyun was shocked.

The scenery along the way was monotonous, and the car drove smoothly. Before long, everyone began to feel drowsy. Du Yiming and Yu Junying were so sleepy that their heads were bobbing, even the little camel squinted its eyes and started to doze off. Only Meng Haiyun sat upright like an owl, staring outside while keeping an eye on her grandfather's condition.

Mr. Yang glanced at Meng Haiyun through the rearview mirror and asked in a low voice, "Aren't you going to sleep?"

Meng Haiyun shook her head, saying she had never seen a Gobi before and wanted to see more, so she didn't want to sleep. In fact, she also had another reason for not sleeping, which was to find an opportunity to release the little camel.

Du Yiming, who was sleeping in a disheveled manner, suddenly bumped against Meng Haiyun's shoulder. Meng Haiyun pinched her with her nails, causing her to yelp. When she understood what happened, she did the same and disturbed Yu Junying. Yu Junying woke up in pain but didn't shout, just rolled her eyes in annoyance.

As the car crossed the Dangjin Mountain, a lake appeared ahead.

The mountains were horizontal, the lake was round. The mountains towered into the clouds, while the lake sprawled on the ground. When the mountains wanted to see their full reflection in the lake, the lake elongated itself like a mirror with arms, stretching horizontally. The slope of the mountains gradually decreased, like the eyebrows dipping down towards the tail ends of the brows. In the lake, the contours of the mountains gradually blurred. The lake, from smooth and round, became winding and narrow, obstructed by grass from spreading in all directions.

Outside the fences on both sides of the road were vast grasslands. Camels raised by herdsmen grazed in the distance, leisurely and contentedly.

Except for Meng Qingshan, who was still sleeping, everyone else was busy taking photos, except Meng Haiyun, who had a painful expression on her face. After a while, she was seen biting her lip tightly, occasionally letting out a groan. Mr. Yang noticed something abnormal through the rearview mirror and asked her promptly, "Are you feeling unwell?"

"I, I'm too hungry and now my stomach hurts."

Mr. Yang originally planned to eat at the rest area because the schedule was tight, and they had to reach Huatugou before dark. But seeing the current situation, he knew that Meng Haiyun couldn't endure it anymore.

"Ah, you just came from the south, and are not used to it yet. In high-altitude areas, you get hungry sooner. This is a kind of altitude sickness," Mr. Yang said, seeing through it at a glance.

Wang Hui also asked, "Do you have a headache? Shortness of breath? Ringing in your ears?"

Meng Haiyun shook her head weakly, "I just need to rest for a while and eat something."

The car left the highway and stopped on the sand. Everyone began to search for their own dry rations and snacks. Mr. Yang's dry rations included a kind of bread, resembling cat ears, and some lamb meat with cumin and pepper powder as dipping sauce. Meng Haiyun took a piece of the bread and a small piece of lamb meat, and she was about to put it into her mouth when she felt nauseous ...

Meng Haiyun jumped out of the car, then the other two girls heard her whisper, "Get off the car!"

They suddenly realised that the time had come and immediately sprang into action!

The three of them got off the car and immediately dispersed with clear assignments. Meng Haiyun covered her mouth and ran to the grassland far away to pretend to vomit. Du Yiming pretended to fetch something, and when Mr. Yang opened the rear compartment of the small truck, she secretly untied the rope of the little camel.

The poor little camel had been tied up for most of the day, still in a state of shock. Suddenly, its hands and feet were released, and it stood up abruptly, almost knocking its head to a concussion against the roof.

Yu Junying had no choice but to pull on the reins attached to the nose ring of the little camel and pull it out. Unexpectedly, this usually docile little guy, after the shock just now, suddenly went crazy, struggling to break free from the reins, and ran away

...

Mr. Yang was squatting and smoking when he felt a gust of wind rushing past his ears, his face itching. When he touched it, it was the prickly camel hair. By the time he realised what was happening, he saw the little camel wooshing past.

The camel ran away? Mr. Yang shouted in his heart: this is bad, once camels start running, their speed is not inferior to horses, can we catch up?

He cursed loudly and quickly dialed a number on his phone. When there was an accident on the highway, you could ask for help.

Du Yiming saw the camel running away and then saw Yu Junying standing in place, holding her arms. She slapped her on the back and asked, "Why aren't you chasing after it?"

"Chase? Do we need to chase? Weren't we supposed to release it anyway?"

"Ah, it's running wild on the highway. What if it collides with other cars?"

This Yu Junying! No matter how much she explained, it was useless; she'd better start chasing. Du Yiming hurriedly ran after it, but how could two legs run faster than four? Moreover, she was afraid of exacerbating altitude sickness and didn't dare to run too fast. After a while, she had to stop and support her knees, gasping for breath. But the camel didn't have altitude sickness. Once it regained its freedom, it ran like crazy. Its neck stretched out, throwing up dust behind it. As it ran, people noticed that there were still things tied to its back, bobbing up and down, ready to fall off at any moment.

Wang Hui was originally rushing to finish her work on her laptop. When she heard the commotion outside, she was about to get off the car to check, but unexpectedly, this movement woke up Old Meng.

Meng Qingshan stared at her for three or four seconds before asking, "Are you from the Women's Exploration Team? What's your name?"

Wang Hui had clearly introduced herself in the morning, but after a short sleep, the old man's memory had become confused again.

"Mr Meng, I'm not ..."

"Oh, you really aren't. Your clothes are so bright, you couldn't possibly be from the exploration team."

Meng Qingshan turned around and found that the little camel was missing, which made him visibly alarmed.

Although camels seemed gentle, they could kick when provoked. Moreover, this little camel had not been fully domesticated yet. To familiarise it with their scent, Old Meng had placed his ever-present exploration kit, which contained his treasures, between the humps of the little camel.

He was eager to get off the car, but Wang Hui stopped him in his seat: "You can't go!" She was worried about the children and couldn't leave the old man alone, feeling torn between the two responsibilities.

Meng Haiyun's altitude sickness was real, but more importantly, she wanted to use it as an excuse to stop the car. Unexpectedly, as soon as she got off the car, she was attracted by the scenery in front of her and walked briskly. She wanted to walk a little further, closer to this vast basin beneath the sky.

As she walked, she forgot where she was for a moment, feeling clear in both her eyes and her heart. She thought of the Silk Road, and of the Western countries. Since the Western Han Dynasty, envoys had traversed the vast desert, their flags spreading like the wings of the nation, carrying the magnificence and goodwill of China to all directions. Faced with strong enemies on the border, soldiers carried strong bows on their backs and sharp swords on their waists. Generals poured imperial wine into springs and drank with their soldiers, pledging to defend their homeland to the death. Here, heroes emerged: Zhang Qian, Huo Qubing ... A string of illustrious names connected different dynasties. The heroes rode on spirited horses, their hooves thundering, until they merged with the sound of camel bells. On the backs of the camels were the people reclaiming oil fields, facing the desolate wind and moving forward courageously.

Meng Haiyun had never felt so sure that she belonged to this place, that her ancestors were here, and she was connected to this desert ...

The little camel ran for a while along the highway before stopping. Its eyes showed fear and confusion. These people had tied it up, then chased it, which left it puzzled. With a burden on its back, it felt uncomfortable. It shook and jumped vigorously, trying to shake off the burden.

"It has already run away, why are you chasing after it!" Mr. Yang said to Du Yiming and Yu Junying, who returned empty-handed. "I've already made a phone call, someone will come to deal with it. Let's go."

Du Yiming said anxiously, "No, we can't." She knew that the so-called "dealing with it" probably meant catching it and taking it back, then what was the point of rescuing it?

"We want to drive the little camel into the herd of camels raised by herdsmen so that it won't die."

"Daydreaming, you're all daydreaming!"

After more than half an hour, the wind started to blow. The weather here was changeable. After passing Dangjin Mountain, it was the remnants of Qilian Mountain. Two peaks stood on both sides of the road, forming a narrow passage. In the gap between the mountains, wind, sand, and snow often took turns to attack, making people uncomfortable. They needed to hurry.

Just as everyone was preparing to get back in the car, Mr. Yang asked anxiously, "Why is someone missing?"

Suddenly, everyone's heart sank. Where had Meng Haiyun gone?

They quickly looked towards the direction where the little camel had run off, and vaguely saw a person getting up from the ground and shaking her hair. It was Meng Haiyun! She waved to them, holding a package in one hand: wasn't that the package tied to the little camel's back?

"Ah, this child, risking her life for a package?" Mr. Yang slapped his thigh in anxiety. "You kids, this is the weakest camel from the caravan; it can't do anything, so there's no use keeping it. That's why it was picked. Even if it returns to the caravan, it may not survive. Is it worth it? What if something happens to you?"

"What happened? How did you get that package?" Du Yiming asked anxiously as Meng Haiyun approached.

"It seems ... when the little camel saw companions in the distance, it ran all the way over. It probably didn't want to carry this package, so it threw it to the ground, and then I picked it up." Meng Haiyun explained casually.

The little camel ran away, but fortunately, Meng Qingshan's precious package was found, and everyone breathed a sigh of relief.

The three girls turned around to see the little camel jumping and running joyfully, getting farther and farther away, disappearing into the herd of camels like a small dot. Behind it, dust rose like a dough, expanding in circles.

The light alternated with the distant gleam of snow on the remnants of Qilian Mountain, making the inside of the car sometimes dark, sometimes bright. Meng Haiyun placed the package at her grandfather's feet.

Meng Qingshan became confused again: "Who are you from the Women's Exploration Team?"

Meng Haiyun just smiled without answering. In fact, she really wanted to ask, "Am I good enough?"

When she was young, whenever she asked why her father didn't live with her, her mother would say it was because she wasn't obedient enough. Over time, her grandmother's answer gradually became, "Because you're not as good as 'others'," and she roughly understood who these "others" were.

In her home in Hainan, there was an attic with a glass embedded on the roof. Occasionally, she would hear birds knocking on the window, which sounds like the knocking of wooden block. She was really envious! The light only existed around the glass, like particles, like raindrops dancing in a space, leaving behind a hole-like darkness. When she was not tall enough, she often sat in the darkness, looking up at the dancing light, hoping to grow up quickly, to grow taller, to become beautiful, to shine, to compare with that "other"—to prove that she was also worthy of love.

Then one day, she finally met that "other," went to that home; that home was really nice, but she felt herself redundant there.

So, when she heard Mr. Yang say that the little camel was redundant, all the darkness in her memory gathered into a sharp sword, carrying her expectations, sadness, and pierced her heart instantly—was she also a redundant child? That's why she tried so hard to prove herself.

She didn't want to keep feeling like she was at the wrong place, like a puzzle piece placed in the wrong spot. She had to work hard to fit in with the other puzzle pieces. She remembered her grandmother often saying, "If you've been living on a plain, one day unexpectedly you encounter a mountain, will you quit and give up? It can not be like that. No matter what, you have to climb over it!"

"Juan, Juan, are you back?"

Everyone was stunned, not knowing whom Meng Qingshan mistook Meng Haiyun for this time. Even if it was her grandmother, her name didn't contain the character "Juan."

Seeing everyone's confusion, Meng Qingshan became anxious and started rummaging through the bag he had just retrieved. Before long, he found the blue leather notebook and opened the compartment to pull out a stack of folded sheets of paper. Meng Haiyun immediately recognised them as the batch of papers that accidentally fell out of the notebook the day her grandfather returned home, the ones she felt embarrassed to look at.

A black and white photo drifted and fall down like a withered butterfly. In it were more than a dozen smiling women, dressed in simple work clothes. From the revealed white collars of their blouses, one could sense their desire to look attractive. Most of the girls had two plaits, except for one with neatly cut short hair.

On the back of the photo was a line of words: Women's Exploration Team, in memory.

Pointing to the girl with the short hair, Meng Qingshan said, "Juan."

Du Yiming leaned over to take a look. The girl had a strong, determined face with angular features. She glanced at Meng Haiyun again and said, "Doesn't look anything like you! Didn't they say you look like your grandmother?"

Meng Qingshan stared at Meng Haiyun's face and said, "Looks like you haven't washed your face or brushed your teeth for months, huh?"

Meng Haiyun didn't know how to respond. What on earth was going on here!

Upon seeing the photo, Wang Hui immediately

understood. She had recently been writing in-depth reports on the history of oil fields and happened to have come across information about this Women's Exploration Team. The photo was taken in 1959, and these girls came from all over the country to support the construction of the national oil fields. They were contemporaries of Meng Haiyun's grandfather. One of the girls in the exploration team had the character "Juan" in her name, a girl from Qingdao named Jiang Juan.

Wang Hui whispered in Meng Haiyun's ear, "The person your grandfather is talking about is a girl of the Women's Exploration Team who came from Qingdao. She was only nineteen at the time, not much older than you."

"Look, I picked up your diary that you dropped in the desert. Look at it, how careless of you." Meng Qingshan took out a stack of notebook pages from his own notebook. Meng Haiyun then noticed that her grandfather's notebook contained a section of a smaller notebook, its cover missing, which is why she hadn't noticed it last time. The handwriting was difficult to decipher, crooked and connected, sometimes turning into inkblots. However, there were small illustrations accompanying the text, making it somewhat understandable. She glanced at the annotations below the illustrations, which included several names and some exploration-related jargon.

She struggled to make out the scribbles, imagining what they might be. The first complete sentence she managed to read was, "Perhaps it's the last day."

Du Yiming and Yu Junying also leaned in curiously, asking, "Can you understand it? Read it out loud!"

"The first sentence in the notebook is that 'This day is the turning point of my fate."

Chapter Three

Nanbaxian

1

No need for urging from Du Yiming and Yu Junying, Meng Haiyun's eyes were already fixed firmly on the slightly yellowed paper with somewhat blurry writing. She took a deep breath and solemnly read the sentence written on the title page once again:

This day is the turning point of my fate.

She flipped to the second page.

Do I know the number "19"? Oh, I do, but now I want to get to know it again.

The Women's Exploration Team, yes, that's us—1, 2, 3, 4, 5 ... 19, exactly nineteen people. We all wear the same work clothes, the same scarves to block the sand. Some of us come from the seaside, some from the depth of mountains; before coming here, some were farming at home, and some were still going to school.

Different ethnicities, different languages, but we all

intend to dedicate our youth to exploring the oil resources
for our country, forever fighting in the Qaidam ...

The handwriting became difficult for Meng Haiyun to discern, so she quickly flipped to a page where the writing was slightly clearer.

We haven't had water for three days. I grew up by
the sea and never thought there would be a place where
not even a drop of water could be found. Every day, I run
to a high place to look out for the camel convoy carrying
supplies, but the land remains silent, with only brown
hills undulating, desolate and dead quiet. The Gobi
Desert scorches during the day, making people's skin crack,
yet it gets very cold at night, and clothes soaked with sweat
become stiff and tube-like due to the wind-blow.

Luckily, there's Delmu Le. This Tibetan girl taught
me a special trick. She mysteriously put a hard lump in
my mouth: "Candy, suck on it."

But, I sucked on that candy for a long, long time,
and it didn't melt at all! Stubborn as a rock. Seeing my
puzzled look, Delmu Le laughed and said, "A little pebble
in your mouth generates some saliva, don't you feel less
thirsty?"

However, my situation isn't the worst. Some people

are so dry that they can't even speak, their eyes dazzle so much that the world feels like spinning.

Deputy Team Leader Lin Lan told us the story of the Red Army's twenty-five-thousand-mile Long March to encourage us to hold on a little longer.

But how long is "a little longer"? Every day, whenever I have a chance, I run to wait for the camels, and time is like a big tangled ball of thread, no matter how much you pull, you can't unravel all of it, and you can't get through it no matter how you try.

The desert doesn't offer much to see; it's like someone drew a rough horizontal line with charcoal, separating the earth and the sky, and then let it grow wild. Occasionally, there are a few sand dunes, like ink blots dropped when the artist got tired.

In this isolated place, the nineteen of us seem to be the last people left on Earth. Just when I thought everyone was about to die, Lin Lan got up from the ground, ate a tube of toothpaste, while someone else drank urine ...

After much internal struggle, I followed suit. Unexpectedly, just after doing these things in the daytime, camels appeared carrying water at night ...

Inside the car, it felt like a collective sigh of relief from everyone, or maybe it was just me. Meng Haiyun's eyes scanned through those blurry scribbles, searching for recognizable parts. Her fingertips trembled slightly between the pages, fearing to miss any detail yet also anxious not to slow down the pace.

2

In June, the basin is always windy in the afternoon. I've never seen wind like this before—it comes out of nowhere, roaring from the horizon like a beast suddenly awakened and charging towards us from the edge of the yellow-brown Gobi Desert.

When it comes rushing, I can't run. I have to hold onto the ruler, preventing it from being blown away. The ruler is heavy and tall. I'm only a third of its height when standing straight. It's manageable on flat ground, but cumbersome when the terrain gets complicated. I wanted to throw it away, but I couldn't!

This afternoon, the wind was particularly strong. I wanted to call it a day and go back, but Lin Lan said there were only a few points left, and coming back tomorrow would waste another day, so we persevered.

My arms holding the ruler have gone numb; it feels like they could be carried away by the wind at any moment, detached from my body. Later, Delmu Le came. She held onto me, and I held onto the ruler, firmly anchored to the ground together. The wind grew stronger, and I couldn't even keep my eyes open. But seeing wasn't important, standing steadily was. As long as we kept the ruler steady, the task could be completed successfully. Finally, I heard Lin Lan shout, "The ruler is standing very steady, very good!" At that moment, both of us breathed a sigh of relief, and Delmu Le collapsed on the ground.

Following that, Lin Lan came over to us and said loudly, "Hurry up, move to the next measuring point! We can't stop here; if we stop, we won't be able to get up again." I couldn't remember how many times the ruler was set upright afterwards, nor how many times Delmu Le and I stumbled and sat on the sandy soil, only to stand up again. I just remembered that we finished today's work an hour earlier than the other teams, and we got to drink water early.

Well done, Delmu Le, we'll rely on you from now on!

Meng Haiyun paused, hearing Yu Junying chuckle softly. She looked up and saw Yu Junying winked at Du Yiming beside her, as if the person in front of her was the trustworthy Delmu Le.

3

When I first arrived, I used to write letters every day. Delmu Le would ask me whenever she saw me holding a pen, "Would you feel uncomfortable if you didn't write? Do you have so many people to write letters to?" Needless to say, many people care about me. My family, teachers, classmates, they all want to know how I'm doing in Qaidam. I wrote about the blue sky, white clouds, snow-capped mountains, and grasslands, but I didn't mention how hard it is. Delmu Le said, "What's there to write about? People say Qaidam is 'no birds in the sky, no grass on the ground, stones running with the wind' (she's very fluent in these few Chinese phrases, probably because she often repeats them to others), you've described it like some kind of paradise …"

Considering how hard it is for the water carriers to bring back replies for me—having to go out of their way to the military mailbox and being extra careful not to lose or soil the letters—I decided to store everything I saw and experienced in my diary!

The weather is too cold (especially in the early morning and evening, yet it gets very hot at noon), so the nineteen of us sleep in four tents. Waking up in the desert's darkness, in the cold desert wind, the sound of teeth grinding and snoring in the tents makes you feel the reality of still being part of the world.

We only have one tea basin of water for daily use, distributed as follows: one mouth for brushing teeth, one handful for washing faces in the morning, one handful for washing faces in the evening, and the water used for washing faces is saved for washing feet at night. Speaking of washing feet, Delmu Le has sweaty feet, and for her, this amount of water is far from enough. Moreover, water sprinkled on her feet seems to act as a catalyst for some stimulating scent. She has a method, directly plunging her socked feet into scorching hot sand at noon. Suddenly, as if hearing a sigh, the sand seems to complain about the stench. Then, her feet wriggle like earthworms in the sand. When her feet are dry and lifted out, the fibres of her socks are filled with sand, sparkling, and she proudly says, "Golden feet!"

This girl with "golden feet" doesn't think foot odor is a big problem; she falls asleep soundly as soon as she hits the pillow every day.

Tonight, a large group of rabbits appeared out of

nowhere and crowded into the tent to keep warm. Delmu Le was afraid of crushing the rabbits while sleeping, so she insisted on squeezing next to me. I thought she wasn't just squeezing next to me me but trying to pile up with me. I pushed her away, grabbed pen and paper, and told her, "Write the character 'pile' correctly before you sleep next to me."

Meng Haiyun nudged Du Yiming leaning against her shoulder, as if she was the Delmu Le who wanted to sleep next to her. Yu Junying made a gurgling sound in her throat, took a breath, and said, "Keep reading, keep reading." Skipping over a few lines of illegible writing, the girl from over fifty years ago seemed to come alive again before their eyes.

Today, all day long, Delmu Le became the source of our joy. When I woke up in the morning, I saw her holding a pen, slumped in the corner of the tent. Rows and rows of the word "pile" were written on the paper beside her. She managed to write the left side quite well, but the right side was written like snot, continuously running down, forming triangles, trapezoids, polygons ... in short, none of them were normal. Other team members woke up one after another, eager to admire her calligraphy, and everyone burst into laughter. She heard the laughter, opened her eyes, sat up drowsily, and watched me put on all the clothes I could wear, preparing for work.

I'm sensitive to cold. Every time before work, I have to put on a fur hat, wear a padded jacket, and then layer on a sheepskin coat. Actually, by noon, it gets unbearably hot. That's when I wrap a towel around my head for sun protection.

But just now, when I went to get my towel, I found it torn into strips. I couldn't help but shout, "Who did this?"

Delmu Le was putting on her shoes, and for some reason, she suddenly sped up. She had just put on her left shoe and was about to put on her right shoe when I noticed the cloth strips wrapped around her feet were torn from my towel. These cloth strips absorb sweat; it's Delmu Le's way to prevent her socks from becoming stiff due to sweat. She, actually … Delmu Le avoided my questioning gaze, swiftly tied her shoelaces, and ran off like a rabbit, ignoring my shouts and screams behind her. Lin Lan came over sympathetically and said, "Juan, I think you're in trouble this time."

Humph, she really annoyed me!

The next few pages were stuck together, and Meng Haiyun dared not forcefully separate the papers. She thought, on this desert where rain is rarer than oil, the substance sticking them together couldn't be rainwater; most likely, it's sweat baked out of the girls by the noon sun in the plateau. She could even imagine the darkened skin and cracked lips of these young girls baked by the sun, their hair blowing in the wind mixed with sand. Without dwelling too much on it, Yu Junying urged her once again, "Turn the pages, keep going."

4

If hunger was a mere taste on ordinary days, now it has become our most dreadful nightmare. Hunger isn't something you endure; it slowly surrounds you, even devours you. Lately, I've noticed when I'm hungry, not only do I feel dizzy and anxious, but my body also starts to swell. Delmu Le is the healthiest among us girls, but today, she rolled up her pants to show me, and there were pits everywhere she pressed.

Lin Lan, our team leader, deserves her title. If we come across meadows on our way back from surveying, she gets Delmu Le to teach us about local wild vegetables. We gather grass seeds, pick wild vegetables to bring back, dry them, grind them into powder, and mix them with our bread. Last week, when Lin Lan went to the team to collect tasks and returned, she brought good news— she said, to solve the problem of limited meat, the leaders had assembled a team of ex-military with good marksmanship to form a hunting squad to hunt in the Kunlun Mountains. This news was like a lifesaving elixir;

suddenly, we didn't feel as dizzy as before.

Today, when our team returned to the campsite, we heard that the hunting team had already returned. Just the thought of eating wild buffalo meat today made everyone more eager for dinner than usual. As the aroma of meat soup began to waft through the camp, Delmu Le urged me to hurry up and join the queue at the canteen. She held that bowl of meat soup with hardly any meat in it, staring blankly for a long time. We all joked that she looked like she was holding an offering for the gods. She looked serious and even got mad.

She said that the Kunlun Mountains are high in altitude, and the temperature can drop to minus forty degrees Celsius. Her dad used to go hunting in the mountains with the villagers. He said it was so cold at night that even if you broke your teeth, you wouldn't feel the pain. But compared to the cold, fighting wild beasts was a matter of life and death. If you encountered a wild ox, it was best to shoot accurately and bring it down with one shot. The worst scenario was if they got injured, they'd raise their tough horns and charge at you madly. When we heard this, we all fell silent, and even the bowl of meat soup in our hands felt heavier.

Surprisingly, we actually saw a member of the hunting team that night. He was of medium height, with a square face tanned by the sun, a high nose bridge, and a pair of small eyes filled with righteousness. However, as soon as he spoke, his nervousness was evident. He handed me a piece of dried meat wrapped in cowhide and stuttered that it was specially left for the women's exploration team by the hunting team. After saying that, he dashed away in a hurry. We hadn't even had a chance to ask his name.

Meng Haiyun was about to continue when suddenly she heard Meng Qingshan shouting loudly in his sleep, "There are wolves, there are wolves!" She lowered her voice, and the three children huddled closer together.

5

He actually wrote me a letter! Lin Lan said she saw the person delivering the letter was the same member of the hunting team who had brought meat last time. I was so surprised. Why would he write to me? We hadn't even exchanged more than a few words.

When the women's exploration team was first established, we didn't know anything, so the army sent experienced members to teach us. Mountains, salt lakes, wind-eroded hills, and desert were all traversed under his guidance. Setting up tents and collecting minerals, he taught us everything.

I'm quite introverted, and I only talk a lot when I'm with close friends. I thought people like me wouldn't be remembered, but he actually wrote to remind me to take care of myself.

Ah, suddenly I feel like there are eyes everywhere in the desert, everyone staring at my letter. How I wish my heart could grow a pair of eyes too, so I could secretly examine every corner of this letter.

I tucked the letter away, resisting the urge to read it.

I deliberately did more work, deliberately ran far to meet the camels, deliberately didn't drink water. This way, while others were working, I could find an excuse to sneak off and read the letter.

The anticipation and tenderness in my heart spread like sand, filling the whole world. Oh, how I wish my heart wouldn't leave a trace on the sand when I open my hand.

A whole day passed with the letter in my hand, and I only read a little of the beginning.

Comrade Jiang Juan, hello ...

Just that one line made me blush crazily.

I wish I could savour the letter like the "candies" Delmu Le gave me a little longer.

When this exploration mission ends, I'll reply to him properly.

Pages were stuck together or had blurry handwriting. Meng Haiyun paused for a moment, unsure of what tone to use next. She longed to know who this person writing to Jiang Juan was and wanted to know the rest of the love story.

But there was no further love story.

6

I don't know how much longer I can hold on. Perhaps, this will be my last diary entry ...

People quickly gathered around, Meng Haiyun's voice was trembling.

In order to quickly grasp the geographical situation of the Qaidam Basin and lay the foundation for subsequent explorations, our exploration points kept advancing into uninhabited areas. In order to save time travelling back and forth to the camp, the tents moved with us.

But today, after Delmu Le and I finished the survey work, we couldn't find the tent no matter how hard we searched. Did we take the wrong path, or did they move the tent halfway?

We searched back and forth with legs as heavy as lead, but the campsite we stayed at last night seemed to have disappeared from the face of the earth. In the desert, there were no traces of people, only camel footprints, those lonely and resilient creatures ... Following the direction of the camel footprints, we searched until one o'clock in the morning, only to return to the original campsite. However, it was empty, with no tent or people. Fortunately, Delmu Le found some leftover firewood, and she lit a fire behind a pile of wind sheltering rock.

Delmu Le fell asleep from exhaustion. My legs went from heavy and aching like being pricked by needles, to burning like fire, then numbness, almost completely devoid of sensation. I lay down beside Delmu Le, and looking up, ah, the whole Milky Way.

Suddenly, the Milky Way melted and flowed like light. It was hot and salty, and for some reason, tears started running down my rough and cracked face. My skin was like terraced fields, and when tears flew over, it burned like fire.

All along, I've been deceiving myself, telling myself I don't miss Qingdao. But on this night, I don't need to hide anymore—I was just too tired before to even think about it.

But how could I not miss it?

I closed my eyes, and memories came walking down the corridor of time. There were clear skies and oceans, and there was my cheerful self, footsteps coming and going, echoing sometimes deep, sometimes shallow.

In order to quickly grasp the geographical situation of the Qaidam Basin and lay the foundation for subsequent explorations, our exploration points kept advancing into uninhabited areas.

I fell asleep like that. When I woke up, it felt like there were still so many things to say. My hair was already frozen with a thin layer of ice ... I must temporarily forget those things and get up to continuesearching for the way. Delmu Le found that a row of camel footprints actually extended along a diagonal line. She said, unless led by someone, camels wouldn't walk like this ... In this uninhabited place, it was impossible for there to be other people, so these footprints must have been left by them. But this direction obviously deviates from our newly set up camp! Oh well, let's catch up first, then figure it out.

But when you fall asleep, you don't feel it. It's only when you set foot down that you feel like there's a stone pressing on top of your feet. We lean on each other, hobbling along, tracking ... We don't know how far we've walked. On the vast expanse of land, the wind whistles and whines, all around us are brown alkali lands, white salt frost lying on the ground, helplessly gazing at the clear sky.

A large crescent-shaped sand dune appeared. Standing on any high point and looking around, one could see those arched sand dunes resemble sharks baring their backs ... And the camel footprints, they've already been buried by the sand ...

It's so hot, so hot ...

At the hottest time of noon, we each collected a bit of urine in our water flasks to drink, and even took off our outer clothes and shoes, hoping to endure a bit longer ...

Delmu Le fell down about ten metres away from me, and this time I really had no more strength left, collapsing on the edge of the sand dune. Without water, my feet couldn't move a step anymore, and it seemed like my blood was slowly clotting ...

I must have passed out just now; I completely forget what happened before I fell. When I woke up, the position of the sun is different from the last time I was awake.

From now on, I have to record every time I wake up.

I've lost count of how many times I've fainted and regained consciousness, maybe it's been the third day ... Sometimes waking up feeling nauseous, thirsty, sometimes feeling the wind cutting like knives all over my skin ... I really hope someone finds us, if not ...

I ... I'm really scared ...

There are still many things I want to do ...

Meng Haiyun saw the writing on the paper gradually becoming messy and shaky, and even some meaningless scribbles. Jiang Juan might have wanted to write something more, but she began to see double, and her hands wouldn't obey anymore—she had exhausted her strength.

The diary was left with only a few lines—

Just now, I dreamt of Mum and Dad, they made lots of delicious food for me, all my favourites ... But when I woke up, there was nothing.

I really want to take Delmu Le back to Qingdao to see, she never believed what I said about the sea.

I really want to send another letter to Mum and Dad.

And that one letter I've been thinking about writing for so long but haven't written yet, the one for him ...

The diary ends here. Tears fell with a thud, startling Meng Haiyun, who touched her face. Afraid that tears would wet the fragile paper, she hurriedly moved the notebook away, carefully closing it.

"Were they rescued later?" Meng Haiyun asked.

"They perished," Wang Hui said very softly, "The story of the two of them is famous in the oil field."

"So, no one found them?"

"By the time they were come, it was too late. The story of those two, it's often told by other female exploration team members to their juniors. I'm seeing this diary for the first time."

"About the female exploration team at that time, there's

actually another legend." Mr. Yang said.

Wang Hui nodded, "There's another version that says eight female exploration team members entered the Qaidam Basin for exploration. They went out for fieldwork as usual but encountered an unusually large sandstorm, couldn't see anything around. Because the rock and soil were rich in iron, the geomagnetic field was strong, and the compass malfunctioned. They couldn't find any landmarks, so got lost ... Until six months later, people found three bodies with survey maps and geological kits pressed beneath them, but couldn't find the other remains. To commemorate them, people call this place Nanbaxian. Of course, there are other explanations for the origin of this place's name, but I prefer this version. Here, those eight people are the immortals in the hearts of us oil workers."

At this moment, Meng Qingshan, who had been asleep all along, suddenly seemed to wake up, shouting, "Nonsense! They didn't die, they didn't die! Didn't they find them?" Meng Qingshan tugged at Meng Haiyun's sleeve, saying with childish grievance, "Juan, they said you died, but I don't believe it. I guessed, did you run back to Qingdao? This exploration is tough, a young girl like you can't bear it, I understand ... But please don't die ... I've been keeping your letter, just waiting to give it back to you when you return, how could you leave your things in the wilderness? Silly girl, you fold the clothes so neatly; don't you see what time it is? Are you still thinking about leaving clothes for Delmu Le to wear?"

Meng Haiyun thought of the book she had just read, *Eternal Monument*; the time Jiang Juan spent in the oil field was the hardest period. At that time, there wasn't enough food to eat, and the oil workers had to organise hunting trips into the mountains. Jiang Juan, like her, was also a child from the seaside, used to eating seafood, could she swallow grass seeds and wild vegetables? Did the fierce desert wind make her repeatedly lick her cracked lips, recalling the moist, slightly fishy sea breeze?

Would grandfather, who had saved the wild cattle and wild camels for Jiang Juan and her female exploration team, end up finding their relics? Suddenly, Meng Haiyun felt heartbroken.

Du Yiming got out of the car, took a few steps forward, and then bowed deeply towards the distant mountains. Then it was Yu Junying's turn. She took off the hat on her windbreaker, her fluffy forehead exposed, tears restrained on her unbending white face.

The distant snowy mountains, the nearby hills, were all sparse and plain. They silently offered the precious moisture to the plants here—camel thorn. Against the backdrop of large floating clouds, the shadow of the camel thorn stretched long and short, silent yet fervent.

Meng Haiyun gently patted her grandfather. She couldn't stand up to bow like Du Yiming and Yu Junying, so she silently worshipped in her heart.

Bowed deeply towards the vast desert—those girls whom they had never met, were truly great, still guarding the precious exploration tools until the end of their lives.

They worked so hard, risking their lives to find oil for the country. Look, how beautiful the land is now—herds of camels, straight highways, and wind turbines spinning like clocks on the snowy mountains ...

Would they feel relieved if they could see this?

Imagine Jiang Juan and Delmu Le sitting there, smiling as they look at the surrounding mountains. At this moment, particles of light permeate everything, gathering to form their hair, eyes, and rough, powerful fingers.

That light and smile are eternal, just like they are in the only photo left from the beginning, forever young ...

Chapter Four

Huatugou Town

1

The car kept moving, yet it never left the embrace of the mountains. The massive mountain ranges, pure and rugged in their contours, seemed to gaze back at you as you looked upon them.

Except for Mr. Yang, everyone in the car was dozing off. The road started to get bumpy, making it feel like riding in a sedan chair. Meng Haiyun woke up first and saw signs of life amidst the desolate land—every nook and cranny between the gullies and mountain ridges was dotted with nodding pumpjacks. These machines, resembling woodpeckers, had a hoe-like head that would thud onto the ground every few seconds before being lifted up again, extracting oil from beneath the earth.

Meng Haiyun opened the window, and the wind immediately found a new entrance, swirling noisily inside. This woke everyone up.

"Are we at Huatugou Town?" Wang Hui glanced outside.

"Yeah, just looking at this washboard-like road, we know we're here." Mr. Yang tightened his grip on the steering wheel.

Here, he couldn't afford to let his guard down.

"So many pumpjacks! Can each one of them extract oil?" Meng Haiyun had never seen these machines up close before.

"They can. The bigger ones extract more oil, the smaller ones less. But they all can do it."

"Where does the extracted oil go?"

"There are dedicated pipelines to transport the oil away."

Suddenly, Yu Junying interjected, "Haiyun, close the window, or there will be dust everywhere in the car soon."

That was true. The car felt like it was not driving but rubbing along this washboard road, jolting every now and then. Dust seemed like a group of aimless spirits, trailing behind and making the inside of the car hazy.

Meng Haiyun reluctantly closed the window. But her heart and eyes couldn't be closed; she was still eagerly scanning outside.

"Why is it called Huatugou? Hua means Flowers in Chinese. Yet there are no flowers here!" Meng Haiyun couldn't help but ask.

The undulating saline-alkali land was occasionally adorned with mountains with Danxia landforms. The brilliant colours of the mountains seemed like a special garment bestowed upon this desolate desert by the heavens.

"Look, you don't have to judge a book by its cover." Mr. Yang joked.

The sky here felt too close to the ground. In other places, there's a considerable distance between the sky and the ground, enough for people to stand, for skyscrapers to stand. But here, the sky and the ground seemed like two quilts stitched together, burying people in a "duvet," often making them feel breathless and anxious. You know it's because of the high altitude, yet you still wonder if raising the sky a bit higher would make people more comfortable. But with the drilling rigs and pumpjacks standing here, at least they could crack open some seams in the "duvet," allowing people to straighten their backs and stand tall.

"Huatugou has no flowers, Cucumber Ridge has no cucumbers." Wang Hui turned around, explaining with a smile, "These are names given by the old exploration team based on the terrain and landforms. When we came here, the ridge called Cucumber Ridge on the way, for instance, was named this way because from above, its shape resembled a cucumber."

"What were these places called before they were named so?"

Mr. Yang glanced at Meng Haiyun through the rearview mirror, his eyes indicating she asked good questions. "Back then, what names could there be? Places like Huazigou were just uninhabited areas." The old folks in the oilfield like to call Huatugou "Huazigou". Then Mr. Yang turned to Wang Hui, "It's getting late today. Will you all rest first? Tomorrow, will it be like before, going to Well 20 of Lion?"

"What's Well 20 of Lion?" Meng Haiyun couldn't help but

interrupt.

"Well 20 of Lion is the name of an oil well. Lion stands for Lion Gully; 20 refers to the twentieth well in Lion Gully." Du Yiming explained as she prepared to get off the car.

"What about that well? Why are we going there?"

"Nothing special, except that it is at quite a high altitude. My dad works there," said Du Yiming.

"Oh, that sounds casual, but it's the highest oil well in the world, at 3,430 metres!" Mr. Yang added.

"I didn't really think my dad was anything special until you said that, now I suddenly feel like he's quite amazing!" Du Yiming turned to her mum and asked, "Mum, have you prepared a gift for dad?"

"A gift? What gift?" Wang Hui asked.

"Didn't you write in an article that this place is like Mars on Earth? Since we've come all the way from Earth to Mars to visit Dad, we should prepare some gifts, shouldn't we?" Before her mum could reply, she continued, "It's okay, I've prepared something for you."

"What have you prepared?"

Du Yiming pointed to her cheeky little nose, "Myself. Isn't having your daughter come a gift?"

"You've done well in this exam, so you are showing off again, huh? Let's see if you dare do that when you don't do well in exams!"

"I never do badly in exams!" At times like this, Du Yiming always exuded the confidence of a good student.

Meng Haiyun and Yu Junying looked at Du Yiming with a hint of envy. Being able to say such arrogant things without being disliked was definitely a "superpower."

Du Yiming turned to Yu Junying, "Are you going to see the little fox?"

"Yeah, my dad said the little fox can now take food from people's palms."

Mr. Yang then asked about Meng Haiyun's plans, "Where do you plan to go?"

"Me? I don't know ... I'm not familiar with this place at all." Meng Haiyun looked around for help, "I'll go wherever Grandpa goes."

Just then, as if on cue, the car door was slammed open, and Meng Qingshan, carrying his bag, got out of the car by himself.

Mr. Yang quickly caught up with him. Meng Qingshan thought the driver wanted to bid him farewell, so he grabbed his hand and said, "Thank you, comrade, you've worked hard all the way!" Not only did he walk away, but he walked away briskly. Wang Hui told Meng Haiyun, "This place isn't big. You follow Grandpa first, we'll find a place to eat, and then come get you." Meng Haiyun had to drag her suitcase with one hand, clutching her hat, scarf, sunscreen, and water bottle with the other. She kept dropping things along the way, creating a clattering noise. But Grandpa led the way as if he were walking on a red carpet, exuding dignity and joy. His steps were like a song, tapping to a cheerful beat, walking with the rhythm of Peking opera, clack clack clack ...

It was around eight in the evening. The sun, like riding a flying horse, was galloping across the western sky, stirring the clouds into a dazzling array of colours, showing no signs of fatigue. The remaining light in the sky was gradually receding, leaving everything around dim, except for the sun that was still burning brightly.

At this time of day, the only things on the ground redder than the sunset were the uniforms of the oil workers. Red overalls, brown work boots, the standard attire of oil workers.

"Opening a clothing store here would be a losing proposition!" Meng Haiyun muttered. She regretted it as soon as she said it, as a few female workers who had just changed out of their uniforms walked around the corner. They were wearing floral skirts and boots, their freshly washed long hair still damp.

Meng Haiyun took out a bottle of mineral water, dipped her pinky in it, and dripped it into her nose. She felt like her nostrils were burning, longing for a drink. Not only her nose, but her face also felt dry. She touched it and it felt as dry as dried leaves, so she splashed some water on her face.

Meng Haiyun was busy, and out of the corner of her eye, she saw Grandpa walking away alone. He greeted people as he walked, as if he knew them well. In fact, he didn't know any of them, for they showed no recognition when they saw him.

Where was he going? Just as she was wondering whether to keep following him or pull him back, Meng Haiyun's phone rang. Du Yiming asked where she was and mentioned the name of a noodle shop, telling her to bring Grandpa over for dinner and arrange accommodation after dinner.

With so many things in her hands, Meng Haiyun had to put on speaker to listen. As soon as the words "noodle shop" came out of the speaker, Meng Qingshan's head leaned over. By the time Meng Haiyun hung up, he was already standing obediently beside her.

The town wasn't big, and there weren't many shops, with noodle shops dominating. The shops were generally not elaborately decorated, with simple signs of red letters on white background or white letters on green backgroud. The menu was similar, featuring various types of noodles.

They searched around, and every noodle shop was packed - just as Mum said, in the northwest, a meal without noodles was not considered a proper meal.

In Meng Haiyun's memory, Mum and Dad never ate together. Dad insisted on eating noodles for all three meals, and his habit of eating fresh garlic drove Mum crazy. On the other hand, Dad would mock Mum for being uncultured, eating seafood and always wanting to eat sashimi. Meng Haiyun wasn't picky about food, but she hated it when her parents argued at the dinner table while she was enjoying her meal. So when the three of them ate separately, she didn't think it was a bad thing; the dining table seemed even bigger. Until later, when she held her bowl of rice but couldn't find anyone to eat with, she stood in the kitchen feeling lost for a while. If she searched carefully, the shadows of the past still hovered here and there, but time had clear boundaries, and the warmth of the past was no longer touchable. She quickly finished her food, letting the warmth in her stomach replace the emptiness in her heart.

A table full of people eating together was still very warm for Meng Haiyun.

There were only three table in the small shop; plus the existing customers, it was immediately full. Mr. Yang came in, glanced at the menu, and left a sentence before going out. He wanted to find a good parking spot.

Wang Hui took charge. She said Mr. Yang had already said he wanted noodles with two pieces of bun, and the rest of them should look at the menu themselves to see what they wanted to eat.

Seeing her familiarity, the shop owner leaned back against the counter, resting.

Noodles with bun? What a strange way to eat! Meng Haiyun ordered the same. Everyone else ordered noodles - braised, stir-fried, pulled ...

After a while, Mr. Yang came in. By this time, the sun had completely sunk below the horizon. After the only source of light disappeared, the wind quickly filled all the gaps in the world. The wind on the plateau wasn't brushing past the body; it was penetrating. Mr. Yang parked the car and felt like his ears were about to fall off from the cold. He rubbed his earlobes, took a deep breath, and sat down at the table, his gaze fixed firmly on the bowl of noodles in front of him.

Noodles are just noodles, stewed in soy sauce-coloured broth with a few chili peppers thrown on top, nothing special. The bun is baked very hard, with patterns on the surface, and when you take a bite, you have to tear it hard. The bread has a chewy texture, and as soon as it enters the mouth, there is a mixed taste of slight bitterness and sweetness that rushes straight into the nasal cavity. At this time, paired with a mouthful of noodlesand the bread soaked in spicy broth, the smooth noodles and the rough bread complement each other perfectly, and with a roll, they flow into the throat. Mr. Yang ate with gusto, put down the bowl, and walked out contentedly. Meng Haiyun stared at the bowl of spicy noodles, listening to the sound of people slurping noodles across the table, and couldn't help but swallow saliva.

Noodles are thick and curled at the edges, served in a large bowl. Grandpa adds minced garlic, chillies, and a big spoonful of simmering meat broth, filling the large bowl to the brim. The red oil from the chillies swirls around as Grandpa peels off a few cloves of garlic, then stirs the noodles vigorously with chopsticks before slurping up a mouthful ... Isn't this the same way Dad eats? They both eat so vigorously with their foreheads sweating, too busy to say even one word.

Wang Hui saw Meng Haiyun's surprised and hungry look, so she put down her chopsticks, got a clean bowl, and filled it halfway with noodles.

Meng Haiyun imitated Grandpa's way of eating. The spicy and chewy noodles, infused with the pungent flavour of raw garlic, had instantly captivated her. She mechanically scooped up noodles with her chopsticks, while popping garlic cloves into her mouth, relishing every bite.

Seeing that Meng Haiyun seemed not satisfied yet, Wang Hui asked the shop owner to prepare another bowl of dried noodles. When only a thin layer of red oil was left at the bottom of the bowl, Meng Haiyun finally straightened up, feeling how stuffed she had been—her legs could barely move, and her stomach felt like it was about to burst.

Once Meng Haiyun had set down her chopsticks, Wang Hui gathered the three girls together and said, "Are you all full? Now it's time to assign tasks."

"Tasks? What tasks?"

Setting up tents."

"What? Are we sleeping in tents tonight?" asked Du

Yiming.

"No, we're not, but Meng Haiyun and Grandpa will be."

"Goodness! Are we so broke that we can't even afford an extra room at a hotel?"

Before Du Yiming could interject, Yu Junying quickly said, "Auntie, if you need money, just ask me. I have a little stash."

Du Yiming hugged Yu Junying, laughing, "Mum, meet the little tycoon."

Yu Junying playfully wrinkled her eyebrow, "This tycoon is leaving soon to see her dad. So, do you need me to transfer money now?"

"Don't be naughty! Listen, it's not about money; but it's about Grandpa's memories still lingering around the time before the oil fields were built. Back then, this place was a tent city, where oil workers all lived in tents. To recreate that atmosphere, we need tents."

"Mum, are you trying to kill us? There used to be thousands of tents here, and there are only four of us, four pairs of hands, and forty fingers. How can we set up that many tents?" Du Yiming joked, wiggling her fingers as if each one could pitch a tent.

Meng Haiyun listened quietly; she knew they were talking about the history of the oil fields. To keep up with Grandpa's thoughts, she had to learn more.

She glanced at Grandpa, who, at some point, had carefully

picked out the vegetables from his noodles and placed them on a plate. After a while, he pulled out an aluminium lunch box from his backpack and stored the collected vegetables inside. Meng Haiyun felt a sense of warmth in her heart. Now, she was beginning to understand the eccentric behaviours of Grandpa, knowing them were due to Grandpa's entanglement with the past and the present.

Meng Haiyun turned to Wang Hui and asked, "Were there no houses built back then?"

Wang Hui explained, "Right, it was Tent City, essentially the first exploration and living base of Qinghai Oil Field. This small city was born out of oil, called Mangya, and Huatugou is one of its towns. Mangya means 'forehead' in Mongolian. What's the forehead like? It's bare, just like the desert and wasteland here. Because water sources were discovered here and it was close to several oil wells, the government decided to establish a base here. That's when oil workers started coming in. Everyone lived in tents back then. Power station, car repair shops, clinics, canteens, shops, post offices—all in tents. So, it was called Tent City."

Du Yiming said, "Mum, instead of explaining so much, why don't you show her some photos? Don't you have old photos on your computer?"

"Oh, I forgot," Wang Hui, who works in the publicity department, had many historical photos of the oil fields on her computer.

Spectacular! One after another, tents bloomed like flowers on the alkali soil of Mangya. In the daytime, sunlight climbed up, reflecting off the tent surfaces like golden wheat; at night, lights flickered inside the tents, connecting with the sparkling starry sky, making it hard to distinguish between earth and sky.

In the photos, everywhere was filled with oil workers' bold slogans:

> *'Drill through a thousand layers of desert, traverse ten thousand mountains of Kunlun.'*
> *'Wherever oil is hidden, we will pursue it.*
> ......

...

Meng Haiyun felt that the Tent City was more like a palace sheltered by tent jellyfish on the desert ocean.

"At that time, the roads were wide, the street lamps were neatly arranged," Wang Hui puts away the computer, "Unfortunately, we can't replicate the past. Let's make do. I''ve already made arrangements, and the tents can be set up on the open space not far from the Petroleum Hote."

The tents were set up quickly, with Meng Qingshan personally handling everything, as if he had done it a thousand times before. He insisted on using wooden boards inside the tents instead of mats, saying that they would serve as beds at night and tables during the day. After setting up two tents, Wang Hui dusted off her hands and said, "Done."

"You and Grandpa sleep here, the others will stay at the Petroleum Hotel," Wang Hui gestured towards the building behind her, "See, it's not far, and we can look out for each other. Haiyun, sorry to bother you, please take care of Grandpa. We'll come to see you tomorrow morning."

Meng Haiyun curled up inside the tent, resembling a mollusk hiding in its shell. The wind on the plateau sliced through the night into fragments, like strings on a guitar. It traversed thousands of miles, crossing the Kunlun Mountains, Dangjin Mountain, and Qilian Mountains, howling over saline-alkali lands, slipping over the hills of the Yardang landform, finally arriving at this small town. The sound of the wind lingered around her ears, even her hair felt hollow, filled with the wind.

She felt exhausted. The bed board was cold and hard, but thankfully the quilt was soft and warm. Above her head, stars twinkled as if touching them would burn her hand. The wind blowing for centuries brushed against her ears, refreshing yet lonely.

Meng Haiyun couldn't sleep no matter what, tossing and turning, trying to "count sheep." Initially, she thought it was Grandpa's snoring that disturbed her, but in her daze, she also felt a headache coming on, her nose felt like a broken pipe, making breathing unusually difficult. It felt like the mucous membranes inside her nose were stuck together, forcing her to breathe through her mouth. But breathing through her mouth made her heart uncomfortable, as if it were being squeezed, skipping beats. Unable to catch her breath, she had to sit up, waiting for the air to slowly enter her lungs. But every time she felt better and laid back down, she still couldn't catch her breath.

What's wrong? Suddenly a term popped into her mind: altitude sickness.

So in a daze, she muttered, "Seriously, just lying down is a kind of sacrifice!"

2

In the early hours of the morning, Meng Haiyun suddenly woke up. She had intended to doze off again, but there was movement in the nearby tent. She got up, opened the tent flap, and saw that Grandpa was already dressed, searching for his shoes in the dark.

Meng Haiyun turned on her phone's flashlight. Grandpa said, "Why turn on the torch? Once your eyes adjust, you'll see it's bright outside." Then he suddenly grabbed her wrist, asking, "Let me see, let me see, did you wash your face yesterday? You girls care about pretty looks. I saved you a tub of water. Look, I've been guarding it all day, no sand inside."

Meng Haiyun suddenly remembered Grandpa hadn't drunk water almost all day, and his thermos was always full. After setting up the tent, he filled the large tub with water, but only licked it a couple of times, refusing to drink more.

Meng Qingshan held up the tub, brought it to Meng Haiyun, opened the lid carefully, and presented her with the cup of crystal-clear water as if it were a treasure. Just as Meng Haiyun was about to take it, he took it back, "Let me hold onto it first. When your face gets dirty like a cat's again, then I'll give it to you."

Exiting the tent, she immediately felt a cold so intense it felt like being struck by a hammer. Meng Haiyun's first instinct was to retreat, but after her momentary hesitation, Grandpa had already walked out quite a distance. It was the darkest moment before dawn, the mountain rocks nearby resembling giant beasts. Meng Haiyun shivered, but with no other choice, she quickly called Du Yiming. Wang Hui answered the phone. Wang Hui was calm, almost prophetic, asking Meng Haiyun to take care of Grandpa as she had made arrangements for someone to pick them up. With no other options, Meng Haiyun hung up the phone and had to follow along. She tried to check the weather forecast, but the screen lit up for a moment—it was around five o'clock—and then it shut down.

"Oh no! The phones frozen shut!" Meng Haiyun had to put it away.

The feet that were warm and soft under the blanket just moments ago felt painfully when they touched the cold and hard ground. Her ears hurt, and even her teeth, cheeks, and temples were all in pain. She wanted to cover her head, but her hands didn't want to come out of her pockets.

She thought everyone was sleeping, only she and Grandpa were awake. But when she looked up, Meng Haiyun noticed lights flickering in the distance on the mountain ridges. It turned out that Huatugou never slept; the drilling rigs operated twenty-four hours a day. This meant that the oil workers had to work in shifts around the clock.

The road beneath her feet was bumpy. Walking on this boardwalk road felt like walking on ridges and furrows; there were bumps and holes everywhere, easy to trip over. Meng Qingshan, on the other hand, walked steadily, heading towards the illuminated area. There, the machines rumbled, and derricks were everywhere. The Milky Way silently spanned the sky, with the drilling rigs under the starry sky crowded together. Stars traced paths, disappearing into the ground's light like raindrops. Suddenly, the hills seemed to surge like waves, layer by layer.

The terrain became steeper; it's so steep that one would slide one step down after going two steps upward. Meng Haiyun's heart beat faster, her steps heavier. She leaned on her knees, stopped, and gasped for air. She could not help but ask "Where ... where are we going?"

"Hero Ridge."

So this was Hero Ridge, as mentioned in *The Eternal Monument*. The first batch of oil exploration workers at that time saw this high mountain and competed with each other, saying whoever reached the summit first would be a hero. Later, the mountain was simply called Hero Ridge.

Meng Qingshan must have climbed it many times back in those days. At this age, he could still climb the mountain with his back straight, without feeling dizzy or breathless.

"All are just showing off!" Meng Haiyun murmured softly. Meng Qingshan glared at her, and she quickly changed her tone, "Is there oil on Hero Ridge too?"

"Whether there is oil or not, you'll know when you see it." A mysterious smile appeared on Meng Qingshan's face as he hurried a few steps ahead. A faint beam of light traversed the pitch-black night; he had turned on his flashlight to inspect the rocks.

If during the day, they observed the mountains as a whole, now they focused on the details. There were countless strange shallow gullies on the hills, like grooves carved by children on clay blocks.

"Why are there so many gullies?"

"That's the yardang landform. Without trees in these areas, the soil becomes loose. Coupled with the fierce winds of Huazigou, it gradually becomes like this."

"Yardang landform" was also a term frequently mentioned in that book. Meng Haiyun felt fortunate; it was like skimming through a textbook before an exam and unexpectedly finding the answers to the exam questions. She remembered the book mentioning that Hero Ridge was once a vast lake during a certain period. Over time, due to geological evolution, the large lake gradually disappeared, and the sediment at the bottom solidified into rocks. She was deeply impressed by this description because it reminded her of Seashell Ridge, and she wondered if she could find something similar here. However, upon inspection, it seemed impossible!

Meng Qingshan chose a random spot, took a hoe from his bag, tapped lightly, and a stone fell off. He held it in his hand, sniffed it, and said, "Fragrant!"

How could a stone have a fragrance!

Meng Qingshan handed the stone under Meng Haiyun's nose, and she once again smelled the odor of oil, thick and sticky. But how could this be fragrant! After smelling it too often, even her brain felt overwhelmed.

"Oil sand," Meng Haiyun said softly. She had seen oil sand before; so this is to say, this entire mountain must be made of oil sand!

"When I first went to Lenghu, it was still an uninhabited area, with no food or drink available. We dug a spring, but the water was bitter. Even though it was bitter, we had to drink it, but as soon as we drank it, we got diarrhoea. However, among the group of emaciated people, not a single one wore a worried expression. Why? Because the oil was gushing. When we drilled a well, that oil column surged out like a black dragon, shooting up into the sky. My, the oil was gushing out continuously for three days and nights, still whistling. The low-lying areas around turned into oil lakes. I remember it very clearly, it was in September 1958, that well was called Well No. 4. Originally, the exploration was tough, with no oil found for three years, so naturally, there were complaints. I had thoughts of leaving too, but since we drilled that well, nobody complained anymore. Later, I thought, I couldn't leave, could I? Isn't this place supposed to be uninhabited? We, the oil workers, came, so there are people inhabiting now."

Yes, the one thing we're not lacking here is people. When Meng Qingshan went to Jinan, to Hangzhou, to those beautiful places to recruit workers, enthusiastic youths flocked in at the wave of his hand. They hadn't seen deserts or vast expanses before, only read about them in poetry like "Amidst the vast desert lonely smoke rises straight, the setting sun kisses the horizon over the long river," so they yearned for it. But when they really arrived here, they walked for a long time without seeing a river, and not even a drop of rain fell in a year.

Kids from the northwest were alright, but those from the south all wanted to leave. Meng Qingshan had to try to persuade them one by one, and after talking to them, a few could be convinced to stay. He was overjoyed, and went with full confidence to recruit moreworkers. But when he returned, he found some more had left.

Meng Qingshan also felt discouraged at times, but what good would it do to be discouraged? In this barren land, people seemed almost unnecessary, to the point where even birds didn'tbother to visit. But the oil workers must have solutions.

Yes, comfortable and respectable jobs are too easy to come by, so who will do these tough and intense jobs? If there's no road, we'll build one. If there's no water, we'll find it. If the weather is bad, we'll hide in tents ... There's always a way out. Being alive isn't just about feeling comfortable; there must be a purpose.

Along the way, Grandfather walked and paused, sometimes tapping on rocks, sometimes furrowing his brow in thought. The two of them stood on Hero Ridge for a long time. Even though Wang Hui said she had made arrangements, they hadn't seen a single person for a long time. Meng Haiyun felt extremely anxious. In an unfamiliar place, taking care of her sick grandfather all by herself, she felt like a helpless baby. At such times, she really wished she could call her friends. But perhaps Du Yiming and the others were still asleep, and besides, her phone had just warmed up; it could be turned on, but she was afraid that it might freeze again if she tried to make phone calls. So she had to give up. Unreasonably, she felt a wave of grievance washing over her. The wind kept slipping through her fingertips, just like those fragmented but warm memories in her mind. When you were experiencing, they were taken for granted, but when you had lost it, endless regrets followed. If her mother were still alive, she really wanted to talk to her, saying, "Mum, I've been to the place you disliked. I think it's not bad; I haven't experienced any discomfort, nor have I faced significant challenges. Mum, if you had come here with dad then, would everything be different now? Mum, what did I do wrong to make you leave me here alone?" As she thought about it, her eyes welled up with tears.

Suddenly, Meng Haiyun felt a sense of warmth on her hand. Grandfather squeezed her hand gently, speaking cautiously, "Juan, don't be afraid, don't cry. Things will gradually get better."

Oh no, she couldn't hold back her tears anymore.

Grandfather finally agreed to leave like a child tired of playing. On the way down the mountain, they encountered a man in red overalls. He walked and muttered to himself, "How can there be a place like Huazi Gou? Not even a single tree! Water is more precious than oil; I almost can't remember what rain looks like anymore ..." He muttered as he passed by Meng Haiyun and Meng Qingshan.

Suddenly, he stopped and grabbed Grandfather excitedly, exclaiming, "Qingshan, you're back! Why did you go away for so long this time?" Seeing Grandfather standing there, stunned with his mouth half open, he vigorously shook Grandfather's shoulders and continued loudly, "I'm Xiao Chanzhi, you went to the inland regions to recruit workers just a few months ago, and you've forgotten about me?"

"Yes, I'm Meng Qingshan, I'm Chanzhi's big brother. 'Qingshan,' it's been a long time since someone called me that way! I went to recruit workers? Oh, yes, yes, this time I recruited another batch of young people for our oilfield. All the way back, I was worried whether our team would fall behind in production competition. But look, I'm back now. How could I forget you!" Grandfather patted the young man's shoulder.

The young man also excitedly patted Meng Qingshan's shoulder, shouting, "Qingshan, you're back, and we can snatch back the first place in the competition and win the mobile red flag again!"

Seeing Meng Haiyun's puzzled and astonished expression, Grandfather proudly introduced to her, "This is Xiao Chanzhi, my partner."

The name sounded familiar ...

Suddenly, an image flashed in Meng Haiyun's mind. Hanging on the wall of a museum corridor was a black and white photo of a young man who had sacrificed his life for the cause of oil field. Meng Haiyun remembered his name was indeed Xiao Chanzhi.

What's going on? Who is this person claiming to be Xiao Chanzhi?

"Chanzhi, where are you going?"

"I'm going to find a tree!" The man's tone was very familiar and casual, as if they were old acquaintances.

"A tree? Where are you going to find a tree?" Grandfather asked, puzzled.

"I haven't seen a tree for almost a year. I never thought there would come a day when I'd go crazy missing trees!"

"Can't you do with something else?"

"No!"

"Will you come back to work after seeing a tree?"

"Of course!"

"Well, then ... I can't find a tree either; I can't even find a single leaf."

"That's what I'm saying. How can there be such a land of hardship, lacking oxygen, water, food, and trees? Is this Mars? From the Southern Kunlun to the Northern Qilian, eight hundred miles under the mountains, eight hundred miles of desolation without a soul. If it weren't for oil exploration, even after another five thousand years, I'm afraid there still wouldn't be anyone here. Let's go home; I'm going home now." The man muttered to himself.

"Wait, don't leave ... Look, have you just finished work? Are you tired? Let's go back first. Today, I will definitely show you some green leaves." Grandfather said as he pulled "Xiao Chanzhi" back.

Meng Haiyun couldn't figure out what on earth the young man had got in his sleeves, and she couldn't expose him, so she had to follow along.

Descending Oil Sand Mountain, Meng Haiyun's pace was much faster than before, as if she had grown another pair of legs.

Just as they were walking along, the two in front suddenly stopped, and Meng Haiyun didn't stop in time, nearly crashing into them. Ahead, on a hill, a hole suddenly appeared. This wasn't an ordinary hole; it looked more like a house sunk into the ground, with a proper roof. A fence made of iron pipes surrounded it haphazardly, with a pile of tin cans hanging on it. Just kicking a stone might hit the roof of the house. But now, a sheep occupied the small high ground on the roof.

This sheep looked more like a roe deer, with spots all over its body, and its tail was a small ball of white fluff stuck to its bottom. At the moment, one of its legs was caught in the fence, and the remaining three legs were stepping on the roof. It was quite unwilling, bleating incessantly, and as it bleated, it kicked its caught hind leg forcefully. Every kick made the tin cans clang.

"Dzeren, another dzeren ran down the mountain." "Xiao Chanzhi" said in a tone of someone accustomed to such occurrences, "The dzeren on Kunlun Mountain have been running down lately, probably we have some fresh meat to eat."

"Ah, hurry up and let it go. Maybe they are also short of food on Kunlun Mountains, let it go find some grass to eat. We can't even get our hands on any green leaves here." Grandfather glanced at the entrance of the cave, then glanced inside, "Since when did we start living in a burrow?"

"The tent isn't enough, and the wind is strong, making

everything dirty. We can't eat or sleep well. Sleeping underground like this is quite nice."

It felt like watching a movie for Meng Haiyun, with scenes that were usually unimaginable. Now she followed her grandfather into the burrow, oh, that cave. Just as she stuck her head in, she felt suffocated. Inside was just a pit, square or maybe rectangular, with a ladder as stairs. There was only a bed made of wooden boards covered with grass mats, beside it was a crooked stove. The only decoration was a safety helmet hanging on the wall.

Grandfather picked up a few pieces of black stones from the entrance and lit the stove. The stones ignited as soon as they touched the fire.

"What's this? Coal?" Meng Haiyun asked.

"This is crude oil, when it's cold, it freezes into pieces. Use whatever is available." Grandfather chuckled as if remembering something, "Crude oil, when it's hot, it turns into black goo. Stray dogs passing by don't know it's crude oil, they think it's a lake and jump in, ending up covered with it all over."

Against the light of the fire, grandfather took out a lunchbox. Inside were some rape greens, a few tomato slices, and half a box of coriander—vegetables collected last night during dinner were now held as delicacies in his hand.

"Eat, they're all green leaves. I told you that you would see some green leaves today, satisfied now?"

"Xiao Chanzhi" held the lunchbox, suddenly feeling a sting in his nose ... before tears reached his eyes, there was a plop: a lamb leg fell through the roof. It turned out that the dzeren above finally broke free from the fence, ran a few steps, and collapsed the roof of the burrow. Ashes and sand fell into the lunchbox. Grandfather moved the lunchbox away, reluctantly saying, "It's dirty, can't eat it."

But he was still unwilling to give up, holding the lunchbox and carefully inspecting it below the hole. Light leaked in from the gap, shining into the lunchbox, where the vegetable leaves were covered with dust and spots. He looked for a long time, couldn't find a single piece without dust; just as he was about to use chopsticks to check again, there was a boom, and another foot came down, this time a human foot.

From the top of the burrow came a series of complaints, "Why did you push me? Hey, pull me up quickly!"

From the sound, it was a girl. Meng Haiyun leaned out of the burrow, "Xiao Chanzhi" following closely behind. Taking a closer look, it was Du Yiming with one leg stuck in the hole, struggling to pull it out.

She gently called Xiao Chanzhi "Cousin".

Cousin? Meng Haiyun was dumbfounded, and these two people knew each other!

Then she noticed Wang Hui shaking her hands on the side, signaling them to pull Du Yiming up and then whispered, "Don't blow our cover."

Meng Haiyun instantly understood, so he was the "mysterious figure" arranged by Wang Hui—Wang Hui had Du Yiming's cousin play the role of Xiao Chanzhi.

Seeing Meng Haiyun's surprise, Wang Hui pulled her aside and whispered in her ear, "Xiao Chanzhi was your grandfather's good partner before; unfortunately, he passed away at a young age. I've read some of his materials, and he was an important person to your grandfather, maybe he can help your grandfather resolve some issues."

"Auntie, we agreed, I'll help you with acting, and you'll help me with matchmaking." The cousin chuckled beside.

"Cousin, you still haven't found a girlfriend?" Du Yiming asked.

In an instant, Cousin looked like a deflated balloon and sighed helplessly with head shaking, "No, as soon as they hear I work in the oil field, they back off, complaining that my job is tough, that I can't go home. I had a relationship before, but it ended."

"I Remember, we'll talk about it later." Wang Hui pointed to the burrow, "Is this thing built by birds? Why would it collapse?"

"Oh, Auntie, you gave me too little time. You may ask Uncle, we've been working late these days due to oil gushing out. After work, I can't go back to sleep but have to come here to dig. I was exhausted!"

"Stop talking now, hurry up and go inside to accompany Grandpa, otherwise he might be suspicious if he hears us."

Just as Du Yiming's Cousin agreed to go, his phone rang. He picked it up, and his face immediately turned solemn, "What? A sandstorm is coming? Okay, okay, I'll go back to the well ... Don't? Go back to the dorm? Okay, okay ..."

As soon as he hung up the phone, his expression became serious, and everyone around knew the situation was serious. He said he had to go back to the well no matter what, and asked others to hide back in the hotel first.

"What about here? My grandfather will be left unattended?" Meng Haiyun pointed to the burrow.

"Take care of Grandpa, don't let him follow me," Cousin whispered to Meng Haiyun before leaving, "You see, the well isn't far from here. If everything's okay up there, I'll come down to find you later, and continue to play 'Xiao Chanzhi'." He pointed, and Meng Haiyun noticed in the distance, the silhouette of a high well frame shrouded in the dust of the sandstorm.

"And Yu Junying, she needs to come back quickly!" Wang Hui said.

"I called her, but she didn't answer ..." Du Yiming raised her phone helplessly, shaking it.

"I'll go find her, you take Haiyun and Grandpa back to the

hotel. I have a rough idea where that little fox might be." Wang Hui quickly divided the tasks.

By now, the sky had turned yellow, clouds descending like stalactites. The gap between sky and earth seemed to shrink rapidly, squeezing everyone and making it hard to breathe. It's Truly frightening.

3

Meng Qingshan stood beneath the "skylight" of the pit, where light flickered between dim and bright, his memories wavering.

In one instant, he was in his prime, with lush black hair, traversing deserts, sleeping in tents, searching for oil wells; in another, he was in his old age, with snowy white hair, every stone familiar yet his territory shrinking, his own oil wells dwindling.

It all felt strange to him: the girl beside him shifting between granddaughter, Jiang Juan, and his younger wife. The unfamiliar buildings and the noodle shops with excessive number of vegetables in their dishes also puzzled him.

Stepping out of the pit, the air was thick with choking sand, visibility plummeting. He gazed towards Hero Ridge, only able to make out vague outlines of hills.

Sand whipped through the air, swirling and dancing like frenzied spirits on the ground, forming into spinning tops. As they spun faster, they transformed into funnels, drawing sand from the sky and scattering it back to the earth.

Taking a deep breath felt like inhaling fire.

Meng Qingshan retreated back into the pit, removed the safety helmet from the wall, and muttered as he headed towards the derrick, "Never bother to call me. Never bother to call me. Stubborn child, truly stubborn ..."

Everyone had no choice but to follow. This weather was like the Yellow Wind Demon[1] from "Journey to the West". Meng Haiyun thought, compared to this sandstorm, the first day of school was nothing.

To avoid swallowing sand, the first priority was to cover their mouths, speak less, and communicate with eye contact. In such situations, they all became tacit experts.

"Where are we going?" Meng Haiyun silently gestured towards Du Yiming, raising her head.

Lion Gully - Du Yiming wrote the words on her palm.

Meng Haiyun understood. Up ahead was the world's highest oil well. If not for this awful weather, she would have gladly gone to see it. But under these conditions, finding shelter was the priority. Oh, she couldn't help but worry about Grandpa ... she dared not think further, only hastening her steps.

Du Yiming and Meng Haiyun followed Meng Qingshan towards Lion Gully. Thick clouds of smoke-like clouds continuously rose, resembling mushroom clouds painted hastily

---

1   The Yellow Wind Demon: a character in *Journey to the West* which occupies the Yellow Wind Ridge and is skilled at raising strong winds.

by a careless artist.

By now, distant outlines were invisible, and the visibility rapidly decreased: two hundred metres, one hundred metres, fifty metres, twenty metres ... It was pitch black, turning daylight into night, barely able to see the fluttering clothes of the person ahead ...

Meng Haiyun tried to reach her grandfather, taking a few steps forward, but failed. She tried again, but felt a tug on her back -- Du Yiming was pulling her. Meng Haiyun pointed to her grandfather ahead, then to the hem of her own clothes. Du Yiming understood, sprinting ahead and almost bumping into Grandpa, she grabbed the hem of his coat.

Meng Qingshan turned around, covering his nose and mouth, asking, "What's this? Is it the game of an eagle grabbing a chick?"

It's a chick grabbing an eagle ... Meng Haiyun answered in her mind.

Surprisingly, this trick worked. Then the wind intensified, sand hitting their legs like bullets, stones rolling on the ground.

The path beneath their feet was flowing, akin to waves. The sand no longer felt solid but more like liquid, flowing with the wind. They weren't walking, they were swaying. In this situation, they had to bury their feet deep into the sand like roots of grass. But with each step, their feet were buried by thick sand, and if they wanted to lift out their feet to move forward, they had to push their feet deeper down the sand first and then lift them. Thus, they had to drag one another and staggered along like ducks, not daring to stop lest the wind carry them away.

No one knew how long they walked. Gradually, the sand grew tired, like a child with an upset stomach, finally spewing out its last contents before receding. The sky slowly regained brightness, as if a piece of porcelain soaked in ink was now washed off ink stains, revealing itself again. A tall derrick stood before them like a giant. If the yellow sand is the skin, then this well frame serves as the backbone.

People were busy around the well, their clothes not red, but black.

Du Yiming asked curiously, "Are they starting work so soon?"

Meng Haiyun asked, "Isn't the well supposed to operate 24/7?"

"No, I heard my dad say when a sandstorm comes, the oil well temporarily shuts down and will resume work until it passes. Hasn't it just passed? They didn't even take much of a break, straight back to work."

The workers at the well, seeing three unexpected visitors, paused momentarily, then one shouted, "Get three sets of work uniforms!"

The uniforms and hats were quickly fetched, bright red.

Seeing Du Yiming, one person exclaimed, "Ming!"

That person was entirely black, with a face darker than ink, clothes resembling a black shell, hard and sticky and dripping oil. It was impossible to tell who it was.

Grinning, he was wiping sweat off his face, his dark complexion showing a set of bright teeth. After he called out "Ming," Du Yiming finally recognised the familiar voice.

She took another careful look and then confirmed, "Dad!"

The people around burst into laughter. "Old Du, is this fair-skinned doll really your daughter?"

Du Lang wasn't in the mood to laugh. He put on a stern face, looking quite angry: "Why did you come up at this time?"

In the past, he only came home during his rest days, all cleaned up from the grease, with neatly pressed clothes. Du Yiming occasionally came up too, but she never came near the wellhead; she just sat around in the nearby dormitories and left. They called it dormitories, but they didn't have the resources to build proper houses on the mountain. It was just makeshift container-like mobile house. This must be the first time Du Yiming had seen her dad working. For some reason, she felt like crying.

"I'm accompanying a friend ... and her grandpa," Du Yiming said softly, in a meek manner, which was unlike her usual self.

"Put on your hat, it's the most basic safety requirement, it must be adhered to," Du Lang said seriously.

Meng Haiyun was busy trying to put on her helmet and clothes. The helmet was too big for her small head, like a wash basin placed on her head, the brim blocking her view, and the clothes were so big that she didn't even need to unbutton them to put it on. Looking at Du Yiming, she seemed quite proficient. She had already put on her gear, although her top looked like a dress, and the sleeves were like long sleeves in Chinese sleeve dances, but she looked properly equipped. The key thing was, her helmet didn't wobble around because she had tightly fastened the strap under her chin.

Meng Haiyun wanted to praise her, but it came out as, "Your head is really big!"

Just as Du Yiming was about to retort, everyone around them gave out a sudden exclaimation. Both of them looked over immediately and saw a rod rising from the well, emitting heat, soaked in oil. Du Lang quickly walked to the wellhead, and Meng Qingshan also rushed over, along with two others, using tongs to remove the oil rod. As soon as they caught it, the rod fell heavily. It was long, heavy, and hot, requiring the strength of four people to lift it.

"Oh my, sir, it's dirty here, what are you doing?" Du Lang gestured to Du Yiming, asking her to help the old man down, but Du Yiming was completely fascinated by the oil rod, only rushing over to grab Meng Qingshan when she heard Du Lang shouting at her.

Du Yiming finally saw clearly the rod in her father's hand, like a freshly pulled-out arrow still dripping with blood, except the rod was dripping with oil, thick and greasy, with a pungent smell. She thought, oil is the blood of the earth, black blood.

The oil soaked into the gloves, flowing down the sleeves, into the arms, shoulders, until the whole body ... Du Yiming finally understood why her dad was all black, a sight she had never imagined.

Du Yiming's cousin appeared from somewhere, nervously checking around the wellhead: if the screws near the wellhead were loose, if the valves were tightly closed, and if the instrument parametres were normal.

He almost bumped into someone by accident. When he saw who it was, he grinned and called out, "Brother Qingshan."

Those three words seemed to have magical power, instantly opening the valve of time, and the face before Meng Qingshan overlapped with Xiao Chanzhi's face once again.

"Always smiling!" Meng Qingshan used to scold him while handing over the half cup of water he had saved for him. Xiao Chanzhi often put his cracked lips lightly on the cup and said with a smile, "I have to smile. Smiling means safety at the wellhead. Not smiling could mean trouble."

But now Meng Qingshan wasn't smiling, not only was he not smiling, but he also put on a grim expression, shouting anxiously at the wellhead, "Quick, quick, quick! It's ... it's stuck!"

"Don't panic, everyone up the well in order!" Meng Qingshan was now like a commander.

At first, Du Yiming and Meng Haiyun thought this was some sort of drama arranged for Grandpa. It wasn't until Du Yiming's dad frowned and urged them to leave that they realised things might be serious.

It was the first time Du Yiming saw her dad with such a grim expression. She asked anxiously, "Dad, what's stuck '? Can it be fixed?"

"The pressure in this well is extremely high now. If the drilling gets stuck and isn't dealt with promptly, once a blowout occurs, the liquid ejected will become bullets instantly, endangering everyone nearby! Although it can be technically handled, there is still a huge risk. Hurry up and get down there!" Du Lang explained urgently.

Du Yiming hurried to call Meng Haiyun.

Meng Haiyun had been quietly listening to Du Yiming's dad explain the stuck drilling, not realizing how serious it was. She felt extremely anxious inside but remained calm on the outside. Sometimes she admired herself. Admired what? She admired herself for being like a goose, even if her feet were frantically paddling underwater, her head was still held high. She pretended to focus on her grandpa, using someone to distract herself from the panic inside, but she was afraid others might think she was being melodramatic.

Her phone rang. Seeing the caller ID, she almost cried out. This was the person she needed most right now, her dad!

"Hello, Dad!"

"Haiyun, everything's alright there, right?"

"Um ..."

"Why do I feel like that 'um' isn't very happy? Is there something wrong?"

"Dad, there's a stuck drilling here, Du Yiming's dad says it's very serious."

"The oilwell worker will handle it smoothly, but you lot shouldn't linger around there, you need to go down quickly. How's Grandpa?"

"Grandpa ..." Meng Haiyun glanced at Grandpa, who was staring at the well frame as if in a daze.

"Dad, if only you were here."

"I'll pick you up from Huatugou when I finish this business trip. Auntie Xiao said you should call her every day, but you haven't. She's worried something might have happened to you, so she asked me to check."

Meng Haiyun suddenly felt a sense of resentment. Even Xiao Ge was concerned about me, but don't you worry about me? Need someone else to remind you to to call me! She forcefully suppressed the tenderness that had just emerged and said: "Dad, I'll stop talking now. I'm going to support Grandpa, so he won't fall."

"Hurry, and give me a call after you go down."

Meng Qingshan hadn't moved, his gaze glued to one spot. The term "stuck drilling" ignited memories for him -- time cracked opened a slim gap while space rearranged itself. He had never grown old or confused in memory; he remained forever in that time of dark hair and bright eyes. Black oil, red clothing, these were the only colours in his life for a long time. Life after retirement was dull and uninspiring. Year after year, he longed to return to the past. His memory truly wove a net around him, trapping him within.

4

Back then, he and his partner Xiao Chanzhi spent over two hours every evening inspecting several wells. He held the flashlight while Xiao Chanzhi kept notes. Due to the high altitude, the ballpen often failed to release ink, or got damaged when it was dropped to the ground . At such times, Xiao Chanzhi would anxiously shout, "Qingshan, the pen is broken and I can't write anymore. You have to remember these numbers for me."

During inspections, Xiao Chanzhi always chattered away while his partner Meng Qingshan listened silently. Xiao Chanzhi would ask, "Qingshan, do you think tall people suffer more from lack of oxygen?" or "Qingshan, why do you think oil is only found in such places? The land here is all salt crust, and there's such strong wind. Why would oil choose to grow here?" Then he'd ask, "Qingshan, they say we'll get altitude sickness as we age. Are you afraid?"

Most of the time, the one asking questions didn't get an answer, nor did he care about the answer. In the boundless wilderness, with only the two of them, they needed to speak;

otherwise, it would be too lonely.

There were often some very tough jobs in the oilfield. Once, they needed to drill several new wells, but without electric drills, they had to set up high-voltage wires on the spot. Xiao Chanzhi stepped forward. With just his mouth, he could command the attention of so many people, and so many hands, and then the pits for the electric poles were quickly dug.

Neat and deep pits were ready, waiting for the electric poles to be planted. But then a letter arrived, saying the road to the ditch needed widening, or the trucks couldn't pass through. The original holes for the electric poles couldn't be used, and new ones had to be dug.

Everyone deflated instantly, cursing and complaining. Xiao Chanzhi, however, fell silent, staring into the distance in thought. For many days, he always returned late, long after everyone else had finished, and once back at the den, he'd fall asleep immediately. One day, someone suddenly discovered new holes for electric poles. It turned out Xiao Chanzhi had secretly dug them.

Someone said, "Xiao Chanzhi, are you insane? The ground is so hard, and the slope so steep, and you dug alone? Didn't you think to ask for help?"

The next day, he silently carried his shovel and hoe up the mountain again. But this time, behind him, a group of people followed ... The new holes for electric poles were quickly dug,

Back then, he and his partner Xiao Chanzhi
spent over two hours every evening
inspecting several wells. He held the
flashlight while Xiao Chanzhi kept notes.

just as deep and round as before. They also filled in the old holes.

People told Meng Qingshan, "You've got a great partner there, Meng Qingshan." Meng Qingshan didn't say anything, but in his heart, he felt proud.

When nobody was looking, he would secretly slip Xiao Chanzhi a bottle of water, saying, "Take care of yourself. When you're still young, take care of your health. Otherwise, you will suffer at an old age." Each person only had one bottle of water a day, and Xiao Chanzhi knew, this water was saved from Meng Qingshan's own cup or basin. The two partners didn't need to say much; their hearts were connected.

Meng Qingshan would never forget that night when they returned from inspection. Everyone was already asleep, but at around three in the morning, news of a stuck bit suddenly came from the well site. Xiao Chanzhi didn't wake him up, but ran to the scene alone.

A stuck bit was the emergency situation when the drill bit got trapped in the depth of the earth as it entered, and the earth wouldn't let go, clamping down on the drill bit. The drill bit kept spinning, heating up like a bullet. But no matter how hard the drill bit tried, the earth wouldn't let go. Stuck in this deadlock, the drill bit couldn't go down or come up.

Xiao Chanzhi asked the workers on duty that night, "What method did you tried?"

"We've tried shock release, but it didn't work."

"What about lifting it up?"

"Oh, the weight indicator's dial kept jumping up, climbing from twenty-four grids to thirty-eight grids, but it didn't move."

Experienced oilfield workers all knew that when the drill bit was stuck, it needed to be lifted from where it was stuck to get loosened. The indicator climbing from twenty-four grids to thirty-eight grids meant the lifting force increased from twenty-four tons to thirty-eight tons. If the drill bit couldn't be lifted, it meant it was stuck tight and couldn't be lifted.

"Then ... why not use steel cables to wrap the lifting sub and drill pipes together? This way, as long as the steel cable rotates, it can pull out the stuck drill bit."

It was a solution, but the problem was how thick the steel cable should be. If it was too thin, it would break; if it was too thick, the machine might not be able to turn it. It had to be tested bit by bit. They started with a five-centimetre one, but it snapped with a bang. Then they tried a seven-centimetre one, and after the steel cable tightened, it also broke after a short while.

Through trial and error, they finally resorted to a steel cable as thick as an adult's arm. After binding everything together, they started the drilling machine ...

There was a sudden loud roar of the engine. The turntable slowly started to rotate, one circle, two circles ...

Someone, not knowing who, gulped nervously and swallowed a mouthful of saliva. Xiao Chanzhi said to everyone, "The drill bit has loosened. I can handle it alone here. The rest of you stand back."

"That's not possible! This job is very dangerous. You can't do it alone," everyone exclaimed.

Xiao Chanzhi said, "It's alright, I know how to handle this. You all stay back, if needed, then come to help me."

The co-workers couldn't succeed in persuading him, so they reluctantly stepped back, nervously watching the scene.

The moonlight paled, resembling a baby's fingernails, faintly. The drilling machines, densely packed, seemed to be worshipping the moon, rising and falling together. They worked tirelessly, enduring the rotating stars above and the sun and moon overhead. Meanwhile, the co-workers, having just passed through an extremely tense night, could finally breathe a sigh of relief. They looked into the distance at the silhouette of Kunlun Mountain, its curved golden edge becoming more pronounced, even seeming to swim atop the snow-capped peaks, resembling a golden fish.

People and mountains waited silently together for the dawn.

Xiao Chanzhi could already feel the drill bit loosening from the taut cables. It felt like an oar dropped into a lake, grasped by a large hand beneath the earth, unwilling to let go. Finally, upon the rower's earnest plea, the hand reluctantly released it, agreeing to return the oar. On its way back, there were deep sighs from below—oh, so unwilling! Oh, so reluctant!

Suddenly, there was a loud crack at the wellhead: an accident had occurred.

Chapter Five

Kazi

1

That night, Meng Qingshan slept deeply, awakened only by the loud noise. Some animal had stepped on the tin can outside the burrow, causing a clamor. He emerged from the tent, colliding with someone who gasped, "Hey, your partner had an accident! A serious accident!"

"Huh? What happened?" Meng Qingshan asked urgently.

"No time for explanation! Go see for yourself!" the person said.

Meng Qingshan's heart sank. He didn't have time to think, just ran as fast as he could towards the scene, regardless of whether his heart could bear it, hearing his own heavy breathing and feeling his legs like they were weighed down by sandbags.

In the distance, Meng Qingshan saw the sign by the wellframe, a monument carved into the shape of two flags, painted red with large yellow letters: " A dangerous, tough, high-altitude task; A courageous, heroic, hard-working team."

A crowd surrounded the area, leaving no gaps. There were dark red bloodstains on the ground nearby.

A square kelly had shattered, with one half lying about

twenty metres from the wellframe, while the other half was nowhere to be found. This kind of square kelly was usually at the top of the drill string. During drilling, the drill pipe and bit had to be inserted into the hole in the square kelly. The square kelly and drill string had to work together to withstand the forces from above and below. These things weighed almost fifty kilograms, so what kind of force could break them in half?

Meng Qingshan pushed through the crowd to find Xiao Chanzhi lying on the ground. All of a sudden, he collapsed beside him, and lost his consciousness. They were both rushed to the hospital.

In the evening, Xiao Chanzhi woke up and said, "Qingshan, can you take me to see a tree? I haven't seen one for a long time. If I see a tree, I want to sit under it for a whole day and night."

Meng Qingshan couldn't speak, tears streaming down his face. He just nodded repeatedly. He planned to take Xiao Chanzhi to see trees once he recovered—poplars, willows, locusts, mulberries ... If there were not such trees in Qinghai, he would find a place where they grew. If one day and night wasn't enough, then two days and nights, three days and nights ...

Xiao Chanzhi seemed to have truly seen a tree with thick foliage shadowing the ground. He sat on the branches, feeling cool. He smiled and nodded, saying "It's so good," before closing his eyes.

He never woke up again.

Meng Qingshan cried himself unconscious several times. Each time he woke up, he heard the continuous cracking sound. Was it tinnitus? It didn't seem like it. Was it noise in his head? That didn't seem right either. He suffered from this condition until his old age.

Later, Meng Qingshan gradually learned about the full extent of the accident.

At that time, the turntable was spinning rapidly, and the drill couldn't keep up with its upward movement. Suddenly, with a burst of anger, it was flung out, breaking the steel cable connecting the drill string.

The moment the drill string got away from the control of the ground, it was like Monkey King[1]'s golden hoop rod, swirling and spinning like a whirlwind. The square kelly attached to the drill string was flung out by the reversed drill string, split into two halves. One half shot out beyond the wellframe, which was the piece Meng Qingshan initially saw, while the other half, with immense centrifugal force, struck Xiao Chanzhi's right chest ...

"Why did I sleep so soundly?" Meng Qingshan constantly berated himself.

It was so dangerous, he should have stopped Xiao Chanzhi, or at least stood by his side.

His partner was gone, but he was still alive. What a terrible

1   Monkey King: a major character of the 16th century Chinese novel *Journey to the West*.

situation!

Crack, crack, crack ... the sound echoed incessantly in his mind, like a clock with a stuck gear.

He returned to the burrow, to that primitive place. He had never realised such a narrow space could feel so empty. The bed was still half-opened, as if waiting for the owner to return. The oil-burning stove was cold, and the chunks of crude oil lay piled to one side. On the wall, there were two nails, one holding a safety helmet, the other empty.

As he looked around, Meng Qingshan felt like construction was happening inside his chest; his blood and flesh were being shoveled away, excavated. Finding it unbearable, he moved back from the pit to his tent ...

2

Now, that cracking sound came again, but it was cut off after a few cracks.

Du Lang's phone rang. He answered, "Yeah, stuck again. Those of you working underground, come over ... Alright, hurry up then."

Meng Qingshan suddenly woke from his thoughts to find Xiao Chanzhi missing. Standing in front of him were only young men whose heads and facial features resembled Xiao Chanzhi's.

"Aren't you going to look for the wire rope?" Meng Qingshan asked.

"No need, there's an underground operation team now. They specialise in troubleshooting underground. Just a call away," Du Yiming's cousin answered casually.

An older worker came over, patting Du Lang's shoulder. "Finish work early today. We'll watch over here. You always talk about making dumplings for your daughter, right?"

"I'll leave when the underground team arrives, and see what the problem is." Du Lang said.

"No worries, we'll watch over here. You go rest." His cousin glanced at Meng Qingshan, gesturing subtly to take the old man back.

Only then did Du Lang agree, heading back to the rest area to change out of his work clothes, which were soaked with oil, black and stiff, able to stand upright on their own.

Du Yiming asked, "Dad, why didn't I know you can make dumplings?"

"There are a lot of things you don't. Come here, let me see if you've lost weight." He pinched Du Yiming's cheek, leaving a black mark. "Hmm? You've lost weight!"

Du Yiming pushed away her father's big black hand, screaming, "Haiyun, look, is my face dirty? Quick, find some tissue to wipe it off for me."

Meng Qingshan felt like he was spinning endlessly, the sunlight stinging his eyes, while his confused memories were like stars, bursting outwards. Sometimes it was Xiao Chanzhi calling out "Qingshan" as he emerged from the pit; sometimes it was a crude pit where a leg dropped down; sometimes it was the new houses seen along the way; sometimes it was Xiao Chanzhi lying in the hospital, a pit in his right chest; sometimes it was a young man holding a phone, resembling Xiao Chanzhi; sometimes it was his granddaughter, looking bewildered holding a shell from Seashell Ridge; sometimes it was Jiang Juan, with a dirty face but smiling ...

He stood there, his mind crackling and splitting like ice. Crack, a piece of the past exploded; crack, another piece of the present flipped out.

Suddenly, he didn't know where he was, what he was doing, or who the people around him were. He stumbled downhill. Du Yiming and Meng Haiyun hurried to catch up, trying to support him from both sides, only to be shrugged off. Du Lang followed them silently, acting as a silent bodyguard. Wherever Meng Qingshan went, they went; wherever Meng Qingshan stopped, they stopped.

Arriving at the foot of the mountain, Meng Qingshan unconsciously merged into the crowd—a river of red overalls, each person resembling a red fish. It led to a bright new building, two stories high, a recreational area for the workers. Many people came here after work to play balls, listen to music, or chat.

Meng Qingshan plunged in and stood there, stunned.

A tropical rainforest!

So many trees, densely covering the roof with their leaves. Easily recognizable were bananas, coconuts, money trees, and various flowers and vegetables. Roses bloomed here and there, and there was a patch of rapeseed. Outside, not a blade of grass grew, but inside was teeming with life.

"This is our oilfield's high-altitude oxygen bar," Du Lang said. "Since the oilfield workers came, Mangya had people; since the oxygen bar was created, we can fully breathe in oxygen. Outside, the oxygen content is only 70% of low-altitude areas, but here, it's 100%. It's completely artificial fresh nature, so comfortable ... Du Yiming, walk with caution, don't step on the flowers and grass. Maintaining this oxygen bar isexpensive!"

Du Yiming exaggeratedly took a deep breath and then patted her chest, saying, "Oh, I'm high on oxygen!"

"You've only breathed for a short while, how can you feel high? I did get high on oxygen before. Once, during a shift change rest, I went back to Dunhuang. After dinner, I felt drowsy, strange, right? I felt drowsy for over a month before I felt better, that was oxygen intoxication." Du Lang said.

"No, I heard from grandma that you did something else silly."

"What did I do?"

"You actually cried looking at a tree!"

"Well, then, I was just missing trees. When I first started working on the rig, I stayed for half a year. When I came down from Huazi Gully that time, I cried when I saw the first tree. Your grandma was worried that I'd gone crazy, saying there was someone who couldn't move after seeing a tree."

At that moment, Meng Qingshan squatted down, reaching out to carefully touch the radish seedlings on one side, then stuck his finger into the soil to test the moisture. He looked at the black mud on his finger, stood up, and bumped into the hygrometre hanging high up. This building was a greenhouse where temperature and humidity could be adjusted. Here, not only did people feel comfortable, but the plants also stretched out shiny, thick leaves in delight.

When no one was paying attention, Meng Qingshan took out the lunchbox, inside which were coriander and rape green with dust on it? He had kept them.

He reached out his hand, and with a flash of green light, he swiftly plucked a cucumber, sneakily stuffing it into his lunchbox.

But someone spotted him and shouted, "Hey, who's stealing vegetables?"

Meng Qingshan hastily tried to close the lunchbox lid, but the more he tried, the more it resisted. His hands trembled, causing the lunchbox to clang loudly. In his urgency, he gave it a strong push, causing the entire lunchbox to tumble to the ground, spilling out the vegetables, including that cucumber, which rolled out limply along with the wilted cilantro and rape greens.

Tears welled up in Meng Qingshan's eyes suddenly. He wanted to pick up the vegetables, but his knees gave way, and he collapsed onto the ground. Tears flowed uncontrollably as he muttered, "Why did I only think of bringing him food? Now that he's gone, what's the use of the food..."

Everyone gathered around, offering words of comfort:

"There are plenty of vegetables in Huatugou now, and trees too. There's no need to hoard the vegetable leaves like this."

Suddenly, Meng Haiyun exclaimed, "You don't understand!" She helped her grandfather to stand. This place was where her grandfather had spent his entire life. The Yousha Mountain was still towering high, and Hero Ridge was still a gathering place for heroes. But some people would never return, and the oil fields had transformed ...

Isn't it true? Amidst the roaring engines of the machinery, the world had quietly changed, yet some people remained in the same place, stuck in time.

Meng Qingshan's tears held so much regret, so many memories, accumulated over time, undergoing sedimentation, now bursting forth uncontrollably.

Such a warm place, with so many trees. It would have been wonderful if Jiang Juan, Delmule, and Xiao Chanzhi could see it too!

3

Yu Junying was gazing at the undulating hills on the desert, tracing lines around the rugged mounds with her eyes and counting in her mind, "77, 78, 79 ..."

Since they parted ways at Huatugou, she couldn't wait to catch a ride to find her father. The place she was headed to was between sand dunes numbered 235 to 240. She had counted several times; her father worked in a house there.

The lonely national highway in the middle of the desert was their faithful companion. It undulated along the slope, not merely subject to fate. It stretched out like a strip of asphalt, laid out there. In the places with steep slopes, it looked like a black waterfall from afar. After that slope, the road immediately eased its gradient. In many rises and falls, the road seemed to have a flexibility, as if it could be folded.

She remembered passing by a place called the "Mars Base" on her first visit from Dunhuang. The driver said the geological landscape there was the most like Mars on Earth. With no light pollution, it was an excellent place for stargazing, and on clear nights, you could see the entire Milky Way.

Whether it was the memory of that "Mars Road" or that she was getting closer to the number she was counting, Yu Junying felt good, and she couldn't help but count aloud. Her voice echoed on the empty road and was scattered by the wind.

A three-story white house stood in the sunken area along the "Noodle Road," so you could only see it from a high vantage point. The house was surrounded by the barren deserts and mountains, without any signs of modern civilization. The house seemed to be thrown there, backed by the desert, and the road undulated in front of it, looking both lonely and aloof.

Since leaving Dunhuang last time, Yu Junying's father, Yu Yi, hadn't changed shifts for almost a year.

They called the gas collection station "Kazi[1]." The workers here changed shifts every four months. Every time it was Yu Yi's turn, there was always a reason for him to stay. In this way, every opportunity to change shifts was given up by Yu Yi. The number of times he met his family was also very few, limited to when Yu Junying accompanied her mother to visit him.

Many of her classmates were like this too, only seeing their parents a couple of times a year. They got used to it and didn't feel it was a big deal. Occasionally, they would also wonder how the natural gas that couldn't be seen or touched was separated, reserved and transported. But every time they made a phone

1 Kazi: A gas production station refers to a facility or site where natural gas extraction operations are conducted, and underground natural gas resources are collected and transported to the surface.

call, their parents would ask about their grades first, then give various instructions. After hanging up the phone, they would have to do homework, and then browse their phones, and the days would quickly slip away with many questions in their mind yet to ask.

Sometimes, Yu Junying felt like the three people in her family were like a fruit cut in half, with one half for her father and one for her mother, and she was the lonely fruit kernel that had been singled out.

Want to buy books? Okay, here's some money.

Like new clothes? No problem, here's some money.

Going out to eat with friends, are you treating? Also not a problem, here's some more money.

Perhaps because the satisfaction brought by money was too easily dissipated, Yu Junying always felt like something was missing.

Until that day ...

That day, Yu Junying happened to come up to the Kazi, sitting in the isolated hut, idling after dinner. The days here were so boring, besides chatting and eating, there was nothing else to do. The sky here darkened a bit later than in Dunhuang, but by eight-thirty, it was pitch black. A few lights illuminated a small basketball court in front of the dormitory, casting swathes of white light.

It was already May, and the heating was still on, making

it stifling, and Yu Junying had to open the window. The light from the lamps streamed into the room. In the slight chill, she drifted off to sleep.

In a half-awake state, she suddenly heard noise outside. She jumped out of bed and ran barefoot to the window. She didn't know when the streetlights had gone out, and several flashlights were poking holes in the pitch-black sky.

Dogs barked, trailing behind the people with flashlights. Because people at Kazi often fed them leftovers, some stray dogs from unknown origins slowly gathered around the house. If there were leftovers, they would obediently wait; if not, they would wander around and gather around the house to sleep at night. Gradually, they formed a semi-pet relationship with the workers.

They were excited now, barking and jumping as if they had discovered something extraordinary, crowding around. Yu Junying hurriedly put on her shoes and ran out.

Several torches shot towards the back of the truck, where an animal crouched. It had fluffy fur, golden eyes, and a pointed face.

A wolf?

Although wolves have been rare in recent years, they used to be common here. They often stole meat from workers, sometimes even coming in pairs—one would steal meat from the canteen while the other kept watch outside.

Old Yuan, who had worked here the longest, once said that he was squatting eating noodles when he suddenly looked up and saw a wolf crouching in the distance, eyes narrowed, looking at him malevolently. He threw the bowl, and like his pants were on fire, ran shouting, "Wolf's coming!"

Perhaps the wolf just wanted to look and didn't mean to disturb, but now it jumped out from the shadows, swaggering past people, casting a disdainful glance at him. But since then, that wolf had never returned. So, was it back tonight? Old Yuan guessed, shining the torch farther.

The animal took a few steps forward, then slowed down, turned its head, and its bright eyes glinted. Not a wolf—it couldn't have such eyes. It was a fox! A small corsac fox with yellow fur.

It started running. Its slender limbs stretched tight as it moved, leaping with open hooves, sliding in an arc, landing softly, gently touching the ground. It ran for a while, then stopped, turned back, looking reluctant.

It must have come down the mountain because it couldn't find food, just like that wolf years ago. Old Yuan quickly sent Yu Yi to fetch some food from the canteen.

"Ah, this won't do!" Old Yuan shook his head as soon as he saw the two steamed buns brought over.

"How do you know it won't work?" Yu Yi didn't believe it and threw the buns out.

Thinking they were stones, the fox startled and took a couple of steps back. When the buns rolled in front of it, it sniffed but didn't eat. Old Yuan somehow got some frozen meat from the canteen and threw them like darts. The fox still retreated. Yu Yi laughed, but stopped after a couple of laughs. The fox slowly approached, picked up a piece of meat, trotted behind a mound, then returned to take another piece. Back and forth, it took all the meat Old Yuan threw. This guy must have buried the meat.

This little fox was so beautiful! Its tail was fluffy and thick, with shiny fur; anyone would love it.

From then on, it would come around Kazi regularly. Old Yuan would throw it some meat, and after a while, the fox got familiar with him.

Old Yuan and his wife were busy at the oil field and rarely went home, leaving their only son to be cared for by his grandparents. When his son was little, he would cry and cling to Old Yuan every time he came home, begging him not to leave. But as he grew up, the affection in his son's eyes became diluted. Every time they met, his son would hold his phone, making it hard for Old Yuan to find a topic to talk about.

Why was it so hard to have a heart-to-heart talk with his son?

Old Yuan asked Yu Junying, "Apart from chatting, what else do you do on your phone? Why are you so happy?"

218

"Watching short videos." Yu Junying casually replied.

That night, Old Yuan asked Yu Junying to help register an account. He tapped the screen, opened the videos his son had posted, feeling ecstatic. Now he knew what his son usually thought and did. But then he felt sorrowful again. As a father, he could only learn about his son's movements through the internet, like seeing him through a glass wall—visible but untouchable.

After a few days, he had another idea. If you don't care about me, then I won't care about you either. He stopped liking or commenting on his son's videos and instead tried posting a video of the little fox himself.

In the video, the fox held a big piece of meat, its wet eyes deeply embedded in its fur, with two indentations above its eyes, as if it were frowning. It made people think, "Oh, such a cute animal, what's wrong with feeding it a few pieces of meat? Look at how thin its face is, it's almost like a cone!"

Filming the little fox was a stroke of genius. Ever since wolves visited years ago, the higher-ups were worried about safety issues and demanded reporting any encounters with animals, even if it were just a dzeren. Reports had to be accompanied by video evidence. So, Old Yuan filmed it for the first time.

Unexpectedly, the video became popular quickly, and his son actively asked Old Yuan, "Will that little fox come again?

Can I come and see it?" Old Yuan was overjoyed.

The little fox came every day.

At first, it was very cautious, strictly following a fixed time and route, and fleeing at any sign of danger. A portion of frozen meat was specially left in the canteen for it, and no one complained. Perhaps, in this desolate and uninhabited desert, having a "pet" could bring some comfort to people.

Gradually, the little fox became a regular visitor to Kazi. After sunset, it came with light steps, buried two pieces of meat, and took away the biggest piece, never dragging its feet. It wasn't afraid of people, as long as no one followed it, it could stay the whole night.

Gradually, Old Yuan stopped throwing the meat far away. Instead, he held it in his hand, slowly squatting down to feed it. At first, the little fox was cautious, taking the meat and running away, but from the third day onwards, it could eat a whole piece of meat in Old Yuan's hands.

The white cat raised in Kazi came out at that time. It would slap the meat in Old Yuan's hand, snarl at the little fox, and make a low growl in its throat.

Old Yuan always held the meat with one hand and pushed away the white cat with the other. The cat often felt jealous and stumbled, but still tried to pounce.

One day, just as the cat-fox battle was about to break out again, a child suddenly appeared from nowhere, grabbed the cat around its waist, and the white cat roared angrily, raising its head. The child gently bent her arm, holding the cat's head under her armpit. The cat struggled, like an automatic spring.

Old Yuan saw it—it was the tomboy from the Yu family, right? He nodded at her in gratitude. The little fox growled at the cat from Yu Junying's arms, fluffing up its fur, which shimmered golden under the light. The cat wilted in Yu Junying's arms, curling up into a ball.

During the days when Yu Junying was around, as soon as corsac fox arrived, she would pick up the cat and let Old Yuan exclusively pamper corsac fox.

The corsac fox caused quite a stir, every video of Old Yuan's was very popular.

Old Yuan's son couldn't resist the temptation of corsac fox after all and finally came. Yu Junying ran into him today. After more than half a year without seeing each other, Old Yuan noticed that his son had grown taller, with a fuzzy beard above his lips.

The wind on the Gobi was strong and harsh. Others wore down jackets andfur-lined octagonal hats. But this lad, he only wore denim clothes. The jeans clung to his legs, making him look particularly slim.

Old Yuan didn't expect that in the evening, for the sake of that little corsac fox, Yu Junying would end up having a fight with his son.

His son told Old Yuan that he came this time for that little corsac fox. He wanted to catch corsac fox as a pet. Old Yuan disagreed, as foxes are protected animals in the country and completely wild. Besides, corsac fox ate things from human hands because it trusts human, so how could they catch it?

His son sneered, "Are you afraid of hurting corsac fox's feelings? Aren't you afraid of hurting my feelings?"

Old Yuan felt a pang of sadness. Was his position in his son's heart less than that of a fox?

In the evening, the corsac fox came again. After eating meat, it didn't leave but lay down on the ground, curling its tail beside its body. Suddenly, a figure loomed over. It was Old Yuan's son! He went up and pressed down on its back, kneeing it down, and quickly wrapped its mouth with clothes.

The corsac fox was suppressed, unable to move its mouth, only able to wildly flap its tail.

Just as he was figuring out how to put corsac fox into a cage, a shadow suddenly flashed in front of his eyes. He was pushed violently and fell to the ground.

Things happened too suddenly, and no one reacted in time. The clothes wrapping the corsac fox were torn off, it broke free from restraint, and quickly disappeared.

Old Yuan's son got up and saw a short, skinny boy who had spoiled his plan, angrilymuttering, "Hey, small but strong!" He almost rushed up to confront Yu Junying.

People could hear Old Yuan's roar and the two children's shouts from afar.

Around 11 pm, tt was already minus ten degrees Celsius outside. Yu Yi was still working overtime at the gas gathering station. He could have checked production reports and spent time with his daughter in the dormitory, but he received a call just before the end of his shift, saying that there was a malfunction at the gas gathering station. He immediately rushed to the scene to investigate. Until someone came running and said, "You better go back to the dormitory, your daughter got into a fight with someone."

"Why is she causing trouble again?"

When he arrived, the two had already calmed down.

Old Yuan's son was panting heavily, while Yu Junying stood by, as if nothing had happened, obviously having gained the upper hand just now.

"Oh, when will you start acting like a girl?" Yu Yi said helplessly and angrily.

Old Yuan's son was shocked. Was this a girl? He actually lost to a girl? How embarrassing!

Old Yuan scolded his son, "Are you crazy? If it weren't for her to stop you, you might have hurt the corsac fox. Trying to catch corsac fox as a pet is just wishful thinking!"

"You never understand! I'm out of here!"

There were no cars back to Dunhuang that day, so Old

Yuan's son had to stay another night. Yu Junying was afraid that corsac fox would come back again, so she was sitting on the steps outside, watching.

Near the Kazi, there were red willows planted. They looked unremarkable, with their branches sprawling everywhere, seeming somewhat unrestrained, and compared to the gentle swaying willows in the south, they appeared much inferior. However, they were the main force in preventing wind and fixing sand in the Gobi.

Once in class, when Ms. Huang asked Meng Haiyun to name desert plants besides poplar trees, someone reminded her of red willows. Meng Haiyun asked back, "Aren't red willows used for lamb barbecue?" The whole class burst into laughter.

Leaning against the red willow, Yu Junying looked up, only to see the Milky Way suspended in the air like shattered mercury. Yu Yi came to call her back several times, but seeing that she refused to go back, he had to bring a fleece coat and tightly wrap her up.

When she was a child, whenever she saw her mother packing her bags to "fly", she would pretend to be sick or intentionally not eat. The more anxious her mother became, the more stubborn she became. In the end, her mother had to take out a stack of pocket money, kiss her on the cheek, and hurriedly leave. As for her father, he only came home once every year or two. Yu Junying often stayed at home alone, leaving the lights on all night. She was afraid and couldn't sleep, so she had to sit at the head of the bed holding the blanket. Many times, in a daze, she dreamt that the bed became a flying carpet, and she floated away from the earth. In the morning, the roof was like a net, covering her, and her roots touched the ground again.

As she grew a little older, Yu Junying was no longer afraid of the dark. She completely dressed like a boy. Her "reputation" had already spread throughout the campus, and people often came specially to see what this girl looked like, a girl who had little words and a tough temper, a girl who looked moreboyish than a boy.

She didn't know when she fell asleep, nor did she know when she was carried back to the dormitory. When Yu Junying woke up, her whole body was warm, and her fingers and toes felt like they had melted. She pulled open the curtains and was shocked. Outside, there was already a sandstorm. The sky had turned into yellow soup, and the air was like a river stirring up sand.

She opened the door and went downstairs. Aunt Lu at the registration desk was on the phone, saying, "What? I just started my shift, how can I go down? I have to stay for more than three months for this shift, don't wait for me, hurry up and take him to the hospital!"

After hanging up the phone, Aunt Lu complained to her companion nearby, saying her child was sick, and it was exhausting for the grandparents to take care of the child alone. They insisted on waiting for her to return before taking the child to the hospital. Wiping away her tears, she said if she could leave now, she would have done so long ago.

Another person said, "Our work here means we can't take care of our families. My child is already seven years old, and I've only spent three spring festivals with him in total." As they spoke, both of them choked up.

Yu Junying wanted to slip past them to go outside and see the sandstorm. Suddenly, the heavy door curtain was lifted at one corner, and in came someone—it was Wang Hui.

Wang Hui said a sandstorm had hit, and she was afraid Yu Junying might get into trouble, so she came specifically to take her back and meet up with everyone else. Then she asked if she had seen the little corsac fox she had been longing for. Yu Junying said, "Auntie, the little corsac fox might never come back again."

As Yu Junying was explaining the situation to Wang Hui, Old Yuan's son, the culprit, walked over from the corridor. He saw Yu Junying and glanced at her resentfully. Just as he was about to lift the curtain and leave, he ran into his father. Old Yuan quickly dragged him in, saying, "The sandstorm outside is too strong; don't go out!"

Old Yuan's son, in a fit of anger, said, "You always interfere with everything, why not let me go?"

Old Yuan said, "Haven't you seen what the weather is like? Will any driver be willing to go out? Besides, it's been a long time since the two of us met. I took a day off today specially to talk to you; don't leave."

Old Yuan's son skeptically asked Wang Hui, "Auntie, did you see many cars outside when you just came in from outside?"

Before she could answer, Mr. Yang interjected, "There are no cars outside. Can you drive in this weather? If it weren't for an emergency, I wouldn't have come either."

Old Yuan's son reluctantly returned to the room.

Wang Hui took Yu Junying back to the room, intending to wait for the sandstorm to pass before reuniting with Du Yiming and the others.

Yu Junying leaned on the window sill, looking outside—no sign of the little corsac fox. The sandstorm was rolling, and the earth had long lost its boundaries and shape, resembling a huge, churning cauldron.

Fortunately, it didn't last long; the sandstorm soon ended, and the world returned to its original state. Yu Junying wanted to bid farewell to her father, but found him back at his workstation, so she left a note and left.

For some reason, the stray dog in Kazi today seemed particularly excited, barking incessantly. After driving for four or five kilometres, Mr. Yang suddenly stared at the rearview mirror and said, "What's following our car? Is it a dog?"

It left behind a trail of yellow marks
wherever it went, with its own rhythm,
and Yu Junying could even hear the beat
- tap, tap, tap ...

Yu Junying turned around and vaguely saw a yellow, slender figure, like a flame, flashing past the roadside, as light as a feather.

"It's the little corsac fox! My little corsac fox!" she exclaimed, quickly asking the driver to stop the car.

"This is a national road; how can you just ask to stop?" Mr. Yang grumbled.

At this moment, a middle-aged man nearby interjected, "It's just a fox; what's so special about it?"

"Exactly," an old man beside him chimed in, "There seem to be more animals around here in recent years. Last year, I saw a den of ferrets in the back mountains."

"Since hunting is prohibited, they're all protected now; naturally, there are more," another person added.

"Why is it following you? How does it know you're in this car?" Wang Hui asked.

Yu Junying speculated that the little corsac fox hadn't left; it had been with her in Kazi all night, accompanying her out the door. Although she couldn't see it, dogs could smell it, so they were barking. When she got on the car, it followed. It must be like this. Thinking of this, Yu Junying felt warm inside.

The passangers in the car were originally a group of strangers. Now because of a little corsac fox, they found a common topic and started to chat. Oil workers who spent years outside shared their encounters with various wild animals. Who among them hadn't experienced a few thrilling and adventurous stories?

Listening to their conversations, Yu Junying's heart gradually felt lighter and more at ease. She turned her head to look outside the window, where dots of green dotted the sand dunes. Although she couldn't see any trace of the little corsac fox, she fully believed that her little corsac fox would live well here.

At that moment, the highway seemed to turn into a scroll, and the car became the lightning moving on the scroll, with the little corsac fox as the pen, chasing after the lightning. It was afraid of falling behind, so it wrote swiftly.

It left behind a trail of yellow marks wherever it went, with its own rhythm, and Yu Junying could even hear the beat - tap, tap, tap ...

Wang Hui hugged her shoulder. The face of this child, who usually dressed up like a boy and behaved fearlessly, was now filled with reluctance. She smiled and said, "You're almost making me sentimental. The environment is better now; there must be other corsac foxes near the Kazi. When you come next time, it might bring a little corsac fox to see you."

Chapter Six

Lion Gully

1

The feeling of flour and fine sand was similar when touched by hand, but once water was added, they became completely different—sand mixed with water turned into mud, while flour mixed with water turned into dough.

Du Lang attempted to treat flour as if it were sand. He pulled the dough into a long strip, then cut it into chunks. Though rolling out the dough was a bit tricky, it couldn't be as difficult as managing an oil well, right?

Back then, the oil pipeline of over two hundred kilometres often got clogged due to the sticky wax inside. It was him who pondered over it and came up with the idea of using a plastic ball to roll from one end of the pipeline to the other, trying to scrape off the wax. And it worked. Initially, he thought it was impossible, given the length of over two hundred kilometres, but after several experiments, it succeeded, earning him the Oilfield Innovation Award.

He shook off the flour on the dough chunks and then rolled them into long strips. Du Yiming watched as the dough became thinner and thinner, and remarked, "Dad, are you making dumplings or noodles?"

Du Lang took a look, and the dough was already in a mess. His mind was solely focused on the oil pipeline of over two hundred kilometres, but when he looked down, he noticed the dough was covered with a lot of black stuff. He tried to pick it off with his hands, but strangely, the more he picked, the dirtier the dough became?

"Dad, did you wash your hands?" Du Yiming tossed aside her phone and came over to supervise, quickly spotting the issue.

"I did, many times, look," he said, showing his hands.

"What about your fingernails?"

Sure enough, there were still traces of oil in the fingernail crevices. He instinctively pressed his fingers onto the dough, trying to get the dirt out of the crevices.

"Oh, it's so dirty! Dad, if I hadn't been watching, were you planning to use this dirty dough to make dumplings for me? You would poison your own daughter."

"How could I poison you! I'll just pick off this dirty bit, and it'll be fine."

Meng Haiyun watched the father and daughter, smiling bitterly. She suddenly remembered when she was on Hero Ridge, her dad reminded her to make a call when she descended the mountain, she almost forgot, so she found a quiet place and dialed.

The phone was quickly answered, Meng Haiyun wondered, "Dad, why did you answer so quickly?"

"I was waiting for my daughter's call!"

Dad must have been holding onto the phone, waiting for her call, Meng Haiyun thought, feeling a perfect warmth, like putting on a coat when autumn arrives. Dad then asked, "Is Grandpa with you? Are you both okay?"

Meng Haiyun listened quietly with her eyes closed, leaning against the wall, feeling a faint chill contrasting with the warmth in her heart.

"Haiyun, do you regret coming to Dunhuang?" Dad suddenly asked out of the blue.

Meng Haiyun hadn't expected Dad to ask this question, so for a moment, she didn't know how to respond.

Indeed, those complicated maths problems often had formulas to solve, but regrets, gratitude, such emotions often couldn't be resolved, because they were like onions, with layer upon layer, sometimes a layer was happiness, and the next layer was sadness, how would you answer? Nodding and shaking your head at the same time?

She quickly ran through everything she had experienced in Dunhuang in her mind. If she had the chance now to meet herself boarding the plane with luggage back then, what would she do? Would she stop her, or encourage her?

The answer gradually emerged: "I don't regret coming

here."

Meng Haiyun heard herself answering clearly.

"I just regret not coming earlier."

Dad seemed to not believe it, asking, "Really?"

"Dad, do you know what saddened me the most before coming to Dunhuang?"

Dad remained silent on the other end of the phone, but Meng Haiyun knew he was listening.

"What saddened me the most was that my home was gone. I used to have such a good home, but after you and Mum divorced, I felt like half of my home collapsed, and after Mum passed away, the other half collapsed ... I have no home anymore ..." Her lips trembled, struggling to maintain a calm voice, she continued, "If you had brought me to Dunhuang when I was young, I could have persuaded Mum to come with us, I could have! That way, my home would have been preserved."

She pressed her cheek tightly against the phone, feeling wet and cold. Afraid her dad would notice, she quickly wiped away her tears.

"Haiyun, let me show you something, check your WeChat."

Dad sent over many photos. Opening them, she saw their home in Hainan, but it didn't look like the ones taken before. Because beside the door were many ads posted, these ad posters were quite dedicated, using different ads stickers in each year. Meng Haiyun hadn't seen these stickers when she moved out.

"You ... did you go to Hainan?"

"I took a few days off specifically to go to Hainan, just to see our old house."

"Dad, be careful not to let Aunt Xiao know, she won't be pleased."

"She knows, and she is supportive."

Meng Haiyun felt a bit surprised, thinking Aunt Xiao was very generous. If their relationship wasn't so awkward, she might have really liked this aunt.

"Dad, do you miss Mum too?"

Meng Haiyun remembered the question she asked her dad the day he left for his business trip, poking at the deepest string in her father's heart.

"Haiyun, your mum and I truly loved each other back then. When you were born, I cried. I think you're the crystallization of our love. I have to protect you for life! Dad hasn't done well, I'm sorry to you."

"Dad, are you trying to make me cry?"

"Haiyun, you said you lost your home, that's not right. With me around, wherever I am, that's your home. Remember that?"

"Dad, were you sad when you and Mum separated?"

"When I was young, there was this hoop game: a bunch of prizes were laid out, you throw the hoop towards them; if you catch anything, it's yours. Life is like this game: it seems that everyone gets a lot of prizes, but in reality, we lose a lot too. Sometimes, we throw too many hoops, they collide in the air, and one hoop will bounce off ... Even if what you lose is something you really, really liked, there is nothing you can do ..."

Meng Haiyun's mind was filled with heaps of prizes and hoops, leaving her a bit confused, and only commented, "Dad, you're like a philosopher!"

"Hmm, I am, and I'm also your 'home'."

At this moment, Du Yiming came out to use the toilet. Seeing her holding the phone against the wall, with a faint smile on her lips, she teased, "Who are you so happy talking to on the phone?"

Meng Haiyun waved at her, pressing her phone even tighter against her ear, feeling like her ear was burning.

Meanwhile, Dad continued, "Aunt Xiao asked me to remind you all, stick close to the adults, especially Du Yiming's mum, and help each other out, if you're short on money, just tell us."

Meng Haiyun, thinking of Dad and Aunt Xiao on the other end of the line, said something she had always kept buried and felt embarrassed to say, "I ... miss you guys."

On the other side, Du Yiming finally found the toilet. It was very rudimentary, converted from a shipping container, drafty all around, and when the wind blew, it felt like it could collapse at any moment. She was holding a plastic ladle, ready to flush the toilet, when suddenly, a sharp alarm sounded outside.

She dropped the ladle and ran out, only to see Dad rubbing the dough off his hands nervously while discussing something with several workers. More workers in red overalls rushed out, as if they had heard a call to arms, ready to go into battle.

"Dad, what's happening?" Du Yiming squeezed forward, pulling at his shirt hem, asking.

"Ming, hurry down, this time you must listen to me!"

"Last time you told me to leave quickly, and nothing happened, right?"

"This time is different!"

The alarm sounded again, and all the gathered workers boarded vehicles.

Du Yiming suddenly had a feeling -- if the alarm was a spear, then they were the shield.

Meng Haiyun also walked out with her grandfather. The old man still refused to take off his red overalls. As soon as he heard the alarm, he bounced up like a spring, saying, "Listen to this alarm, it's a big deal!"

As expected, she and her grandfather were stopped again.

Du Lang said, "You should know the meaning of this alarm, right?"

Meng Qingshan said, "I do, it's an alarm for blowout. I wonder which well it is?"

"It's Well 336 of Lion, a key exploration well. It's urgent

now, we have to go up immediately." Du Lang pointed to the workers in the car, everyone was waiting for him, "In this situation, people of your age shouldn't go, especially with a child."

That's when Du Yiming spoke up: "Dad, you shouldn't rush up there either. You're also taking the child."

"Don't talk nonsense. I'm the engineer here, the team leader. How can I retreat at a time like this? You quickly follow them and go down the mountain!" Du Lang shouted sternly.

Du Yiming had never seen her dad so angry before, instinctively taking a step back, stunned. But her dad's gaze softened immediately, he reached out, wiping her face. It was the grease from when he pinched her cheeks. When he spoke again, his tone had softened like newly sprouted grass.

It wasn't until their car drove far away that Du Yiming remembered she hadn't asked what "blowout" meant, so she turned to Meng Qingshan.

Meng Qingshan raised a finger: "Blowout is ... is ..."

It was right on the tip of his tongue, he had prepared to explain everything confidently, but why couldn't he remember anything?

He looked at Meng Haiyun, blinked, and said, "Juan, I remember I told you, you tell her."

Meng Haiyun had to dig out the book *Eternal Monument* from her bag again, flipping through to find the word "blowout," but she couldn't find it from start to finish.

"Forget it, forget it, can't rely on you, or it will be too late."

Du Yiming took out her phone to search, glanced at it a few times, then put it away. Meng Haiyun asked, "Did you find it?"

"Um, I understand."

"Tell me what you found."

At this moment, Du Yiming demonstrated her typical ability as a good student: "Blowout is when, during drilling, underground fluids surge up along the wellbore. The pressure at the wellhead suddenly increases, and even a nail-sized area can experience hundreds of kilograms of pressure. In such cases, the steel plate covering the wellhead may even be forced to squeak."

"Why does a blowout happen? It doesn't happen with every well, does it?" Meng Haiyun asked.

"There are many reasons for blowouts, such as inaccurate control of formation pressure, low drilling fluid density, incomplete filling of mud during drilling, etc. The fundamental reason is the loss of pressure balance inside the well, where the pressure inside the well is less than the formation pressure." Du Yiming explained confidently, and Meng Haiyun felt she was shining.

"Wow, you remembered all that with just a glance?"

Meng Haiyun thought to herself, what kind of brain does Du Yiming have, is it like a scanner, just a glance and all the information is stored?

"Oh, no, that whole bunch of stuff I just remembered was things my mum told me when she took me to visit the petroleum museum. These things are her expertise. It would've been better if she were here." Du Yiming said.

"Isn't your mum a journalist?" Meng Haiyun asked.

"My mum graduated from the Petroleum University. She was just interning at the Qinghai Oilfield at the time, but then she met my dad and didn't want to leave. She used to work in Huatugou, where her superiors noticed her good writing skills and asked her to work in publicity, so she stayed in Dunhuang." Du Yiming suddenly remembered that her dad asked her to call her mum, so she took out her phone and went to the side.

"I've always wanted to ask, that ... blowout accident, could ... could it lead to deaths?" Meng Haiyun took over the conversation.

"Generally, if handled promptly, it won't. But if there's poisonous gas, then it's aweful." Meng Qingshan said.

His memory seemed to be hit or miss, having difficulties with more complex matters but doing alright with simpler ones.

"Poisonous gas? Why would there be poisonous gas?"

"Have you noticed there's a flame on top of oil wells?"

Meng Haiyun nodded.

"That's called a flare. Along with oil, natural gas comes up, but sometimes there can be poisonous gases, like hydrogen sulfide, which needs to be burned off."

Meng Haiyun immediately opened her phone and searched for hydrogen sulfide. Online it was explained like this: when the concentration of hydrogen sulfide in the air reaches a certain level, in fifteen minutes people lose their sense of smell, in twenty minutes their throat starts to burn, and their heartbeat accelerates. At higher concentrations, people immediately lose consciousness and stop breathing.

Meng Haiyun shuddered.

She looked towards Lion Gully, where it was no longer just a landscape of ravines and mountains, but also a dangerous battlefield. Du Yiming's dad and his colleagues faced such dangers every day, but they seemed fearless, knowing exactly what to do. They must have the experience and confidence to handle it well.

Actually, when searching earlier, Meng Haiyun also saw several cases of townsfolk being poisoned due to hydrogen sulphide diffusion. She couldn't help but think, what if the whole Huatugou was covered in toxic gas? Would Dad rush to save her no matter what? Would he realise that she was the precious one he's been ignoring all along?

Dad said he's her forever "home". If "home" knew that people from the homey was in danger, how worried and scared it would be! Thinking about this, she felt a bit comforted, but soon the resentment towards Dad surged up in her heart, both resisting and contending with each other, turning her heart into a battlefield.

She shook her head, trying to shake off these messy thoughts. Meanwhile, Du Yiming hadn't finished her call yet. She could only hear her jokingly asking, "What? Stinky eggs? Mum, why are you suddenly talking about stinky eggs?"

Du Yiming kept looking at his phone, shouting impatiently, "Hello? Hello?" Finally, she hung up, grumbling, "What a rubbish signal, there's no voice again!"

Meng Haiyun glanced at her own phone, the signal was also intermittent. These days she had realised—the phone barely had one or two bars of signal in high places, none at all in low areas, and the signal just disappeared without warning. It's infuriating! At night, the phone would freeze and crash, she had to tuck it into her clothes for a while, then use all ten fingers to rub the brick-like screen.

"Let's go up," Meng Haiyun heard Grandpa muttering beside her.

"Grandpa, where are you going?" she asked.

"Up to the well, to check some data," he replied.

"Checking data up at the well?" Meng Haiyun was puzzled.

Du Yiming said, "Do you think your grandpa means going to the data room upstairs? There are records for each well in the lounge beside the well, I've seen them, all stacked up over there."

Meng Haiyun turned to her grandpa and asked, "Is that so,

Grandpa?"

Like a stubborn child, Grandpa repeated, "Go up, up to the well."

"Alright, alright, I'll accompany you," Meng Haiyun said, patting her grandpa's hand reassuringly.

Du Yiming immediately intervened, "No, you can't. My dad just said the automatic relief device malfunctioned, they have to manually press the well, it's very dangerous now. He told us to leave Huatugou immediately. My mum asked us to wait here for her to pick us up."

Grandpa pursed his lips, his stubbornness resurfacing, with a look that said, "If I say up, we go up." Seeing this, Meng Haiyun had to come up with a compromise. She asked Du Yiming to stay put while she accompanied her grandpa to Hero Ridge. When the car arrived, Du Yiming would call, and they'd come down together. There's nothing to do here anyway, might as well let Grandpa search for some data, maybe they'd discover something.

Du Yiming was worried, "Grandpa, you're quite old, going up and down like this, what if you get exhausted?"

Grandpa immediately blushed, stiffened his neck and shouted, "Who's old? Who's old? I can eat three steamed buns and three bowls of noodles, can you?"

Du Yiming quickly conceded, "No, I can't, I can't eat that much."

"Then don't bother about me. Whoever eats more, makes the decisions."

There's no reasoning with such stubbornness. Meng Haiyun had no choice but to accompany her grandpa up Hero Ridge once again.

2

The view from the data room was quite impressive, you could see the Kunlun Mountains just by raising your head. The snow-capped peaks on the mountains were separated from the sky by a thin line. That line seemed to be constantly changing subtly, sometimes golden, sometimes neon, sometimes a faint blue, like a veil, changing with the mood of the mountains. The wellhead stood tall in the distance, and you could see a group of workers in red overalls bustling about.

The bookshelves in the data room were neatly arranged with bound volumes of documents. Indeed, there were geological structure data that Grandpa was looking for. He immediately pulled a chair, sat down, and buried himself in it. His demeanor was like a starving person invited a feast, not even bothering to chew, just wanting to swallow it whole. Meng Haiyun stared blankly as Grandpa flipped through the pages rapidly, his fingers blurring into a flesh-coloured haze in the air, the movement of his joints invisible, like a martial arts master in a fight scene. So impressive—Grandpa wasn't messing around at all.

He muttered while gesturing, "Why is the pressure so high?"

"Huh?" Meng Haiyun didn't catch it clearly.

Although Grandpa was talking to himself, his hands were busy, his fingers becoming like wheels, running back and forth on the paper, "This well, it was planned to drill to six thousand metres deep, but it struck oil at over four thousand metres. At the same depth, the density of the drilling fluid was only 1.3 grams per cubic centimetre at the beginning, how come it rose to over 1.8 grams per cubic centimetre in a few days?"

Grandpa seemed exceptionally clear-headed at the moment. It seems his condition fluctuated and when it came to matters related to oil, Grandpa was reliable.

But when he explained these things to her, all she wanted to do was wail, "I ... don't understand, I don't understand!"

"It seems there's a deviation between the geological structure and our estimation. What if it's over 2 grams per cubic centimetre?"

Meng Haiyun couldn't wait any longer. She quietly slipped out of the cabin and soon found herself at the wellhead, where she bumped into Du Yiming's cousin, and the two exchanged puzzled looks.

Cousin asked, "Didn't you go down? Why did you come back up? Wherever there's trouble, that's where you run to?" He glanced behind Meng Haiyun, "Where's my sister?"

"She didn't come up."

"Oh, that's fine, she's good. But what about you?"

"I came up with my grandfather sa." Meng Haiyun spoke with an word handle.

"Are you crazy, both of you! What are you doing here?"

"He came to look at geological data. He thinks there might be an error in the geological structure estimation and he's researching it there."

"Hurry up and go down! Oh, you two are such troublemakers. If I could leave, I would definitely personally send you both down."

"I'll take him down after my grandfather finishes looking at the data. I also don't want to cause trouble for you all."

"Did your grandfather figure out something?"

"He mentioned something about density, cubic centimetres, I really didn't understand. He also mentioned a few numbers, the first two were around one point something grams, and the last one was a little over two grams."

"Was he talking about drilling fluid density?"

"Yes, yes, it was about the drilling fluid."

"Do you remember if he said it was around two point something grams?"

"I don't remember ..."

"I need to go ask now. According to what he said, adjusting the drilling fluid density slightly could make a difference!"

Meng Haiyun perked up at this.

Following her grandfather's idea, they raised the drilling fluid density to 2.3 grams per cubic centimetre, and then injected mud into it.

The workers in red overalls orderly stepped back, leaving only ten people. Cousin ran over and urged her to quickly take her grandfather down the mountain, saying the oil well was about to blow.

Meng Haiyun didn't know what "blow" meant, looking indifferent, which infuriated Cousin. Ignorance is bliss indeed!

Down the mountain, Du Yiming finally saw her mother and Yu Junying. Once the car was parked, Mr. Yang noticed the absence of a girl. Du Yiming explained about the oil well overflow and Meng Haiyun going back up the mountain with her grandfather. Upon hearing this, Mr. Yang exclaimed, "What? That girl is still on the mountain? If it blows, she will be hurt?"

"Does an overflow always have to be blown out? Why would blowing out hurt someone?" Du Yiming also didn't understand.

"As long as there's gas in the well, it must be blown out. Blowing out releases the pressure inside the well. Blowing out, what do you think blows out? Fire, it's fire!" Mr. Yang pointed to his face, revealing a clear and ferocious scar to Du Yiming, "See it? That's what happens when it blows out and catches fire!"

Du Yiming was terrified, stuttering, "Y-you, you also

worked on an oil well?"

"Near the oil field, who haven't worked on an oil well? If it weren't for the injury, I wouldn't have come down ..."

Du Yiming finally understood the seriousness of the situation. Not only her, even Wang Hui learned for the first time how Mr. Yang got the scar on his face.

At the moment, they were extremely anxious.

"Du Yiming, didn't I tell you to take care of Meng Haiyun and her grandfather?" Wang Hui also started to panic.

"I advised them not to go up, but they didn't listen! Mum, don't blame me for now, quickly find a way to get them down, and also ask my dad to come down quickly." Du Yiming's voice trembled with urgency.

"Did you try calling Haiyun?"

"I did, but couldn't get through. Maybe there's no signal again."

"Your dad won't come down, that's his work. No matter how dangerous it gets, he won't back down! We need to find a way to get Meng Haiyun and her grandfather out of here. By the way, have you smelled the air? Does it smell like rotten eggs?"

"Rotten eggs? What do you mean?"

"Yes, yes!" Mr. Yang gave a thumbs-up to Wang Hui. "You're very thoughtful!" Then, he explained to the puzzled Du Yiming, "The most famous toxic gas in the well is hydrogen sulfide. It has a stench like rotten eggs. Once you smell it, run upwind immediately."

Du Yiming finally understood, sniffed a few times, and said, "I haven't smelled it."

"That's good." Mr. Yang let out a long sigh of relief.

3

The so-called gas release, in Meng Haiyun's eyes, looked more like a fountain performance. She hid in the shed, holding binoculars, watching with relish. Look, a stream of water spurted out diagonally, like a whale surfacing to breathe. The water column made a strange sound, churning like a water sleeve in the air, and when its momentum weakened, it fell into a prepared container.

Meng Haiyun found it strange: "Why bother catching it in a container when it's deliberately released?"

"There's oil mixed in the water, we can't let a drop of oil touch the ground," her cousin explained.

As soon as the water fell into the container, fire eagerly spewed out of the nozzle, looking a bit impatient. Orange tongues of fire surged out in clusters. The flames were tall, greedily licking the surrounding air. With each lick, the orange body expanded. The edges of the fire turned red, the centre golden yellow, and the flames at the front resembled a phoenix soaring.

The well pressure dropped. After the gas release, the well

Orange tongues of fire surged out in clusters. The flames were tall, greedily licking the surrounding air.

needed to be shut down. Du Lang pressed a button. This device was called the wellhead sealing remote control console. Once the well was sealed, the danger would be averted. Soon, people remembered Meng Qingshan and began giving him thumbs-up. Before long, those responsible for the gas release began to return to the shed. The fire continued to burn, like a tireless child showing off its newly learned tricks.

More and more people crowded into the shed to rest, and Meng Haiyun smelled a strange odor.

"It smells like rotten eggs." Meng Qingshan, who was organizing documents nearby, also smelled it. He sniffed a few times and asked urgently, "Are there hydrogen sulfide detectors and gas masks here?" The expressions of the people around him changed immediately, as if the sunny weather had suddenly turned into a harsh winter. They all knew that the smell of rotten eggs was the smell of hydrogen sulfide, but there had never been a gas leak accident in the Qinghai oilfield, and his reminder alarmed everyone.

"Yes, yes, we have them all in the toolbox." Someone hurried over to fetch them.

"Everyone else, evacuate!"

" Nothing's going to happen, right? I've been working here for nearly twenty years, and I've never heard of a hydrogen sulfide leak from any well!" Some people harboured a sense of luck.

Immediately, someone shouted, "Shut up! If there really is a hydrogen sulfide leak, not only will everyone in this room be in danger, but the entire Huatugou will be affected! If something happens, can you be the responsible for it?"

That person immediately fell silent.

Everyone quickly put on gas masks. After a commotion, everyone retreated to a hilltop several hundred metres away.

Only Du Lang went the opposite way, back to the platform. He put on his gas mask and prepared to test the hydrogen sulfide with a detector. As soon as he touched the wellhead, the instrument emitted a piercing alarm, indicating that the concentration of hydrogen sulfide at the wellhead was dangerously high.

Du Lang thought to himself, "This is bad."

The wellhead was high up and upwind. If the wind suddenly picked up, the poisonous gas would blow downhill, affecting the entire Huatugou. What's even more terrifying was that hydrogen sulfide could prevent the well from being successfully shut down because, over time, the wellhead would corrode due to the high temperature. Thinking of this, every nerve in his body tensed up.

He picked up his phone and dialed the safety centre's number. After reporting the situation, he dialed Wang Hui's number. When the call connected, his voice was trembling, "Wife ..."

"Hello, Dad, it's me."

Du Yiming held the phone with one hand and pointed at the receiver with the other, silently mouthing to her mother: My dad.

Wang Hui was taking photos. In the event of an accident, she had to prepare for a report.

Du Lang urgently said, "Quick, let your mum talk!"

Normally, Du Yiming would have teased her father a bit, but she sensed that something was wrong and quickly ran over to hand the phone to her mother.

Wang Hui took the phone, initially surprised, then frightened, and finally panicked. Du Lang asked her to quickly call the government department of Huatugou, evacuate the people. Because hydrogen sulfide might spread, and he had to stay at the well until it was completely under control.

Wang Hui looked at the billowing smoke on the mountain in the distance, her heart filled with worry, fear, and anxiety. Although she had made the call and knew that the government department had received the news and had sent out rescue teams immediately, and the evacuation notice had been issued, she still couldn't help but worry about the people on the mountain and below.

The noodle shop keepers, small business owners, passing-by drivers, as well as those visiting relatives or tourists, all rushed out. Some were thinking about the pickled vegetables at home, some had just kneaded the dough to make noodles, and others were chatting with their families.

Suddenly, many large vehicles appeared in the small town. Emergency fracturing trucks and engineering vehicles carrying well pressure equipment passed by one after another, their massive bodies and dazzling red colours signaling the urgency of the situation. Buses for evacuating the masses also arrived, filling up with people and leaving one after another.

Wang Hui asked Mr. Yang to take Du Yiming and Yu Junying back to Dunhuang, while she stayed behind for on-site reporting.

"If Meng Haiyun doesn't come back, we won't leave. We came together, so we leave together. We can't leave anyone behind! Besides, neither you nor my dad are leaving. We're a family ... and we should stay together," Du Yiming said.

Wang Hui usually avoided the word "death." Although Du Yiming omitted that word, it still angered her.

"What nonsense are you talking about? Keep your mouth shut!" Wang Hui said, her face turning pale with anger.

4

The rescue vehicles arrived at the mountains. Fracturing trucks were filled with mud, ready to be pumped into the oil well. And engineering vehicles brought a new set of fracturing equipment because the existing equipment on the oil well was no longer sufficient.

Meng Haiyun asked Du Yiming's cousin, "What is this mud for?"

"It's for well pressure. The mud density is calculated so that the pressure of the mud column in the well is slightly higher than the pressure of the oil layer, just a little bit," he explained, pinching his thumb against his index finger, revealing a crescent-shaped fingernail. "This way, we can control the well's pressure without crushing the oil layer."

Du Lang walked over and glared at him, " Now we are having an emergency! Stop talking nonsense."

"It's not nonsense," he muttered softly.

"He's right, it's educational!" Meng Haiyun added.

Du Lang held a notepad and assigned tasks to specific individuals. When his gaze fell on the last item, he seemed to be asking a question to himself, "Go to the site to lay down the well pressure piping and install the well pressure equipment." He looked up at the remaining people, "Who's going?"

Everyone knew in their hearts that if the fire intensified when igniting the well, if there was a slight problem with the gas masks ...

Du Lang bit his lip and said, "I'll go!" He handed the notepad to Du Yiming's cousin and instructed, "Stay here, track the progress of the tasks listed above, and stay in touch with me at all times."

"No, I can't be the commander-in-chief!" Du Yiming's cousin's face turned red with anxiety. "Tell me the main points, and I'll give it a try."

"You can't try this. It has to be successful at once. Young man, it's times like these when us old hands are more reliable." an older worker with half-grey hair said, pulling Du Yiming's cousin back and pushing him forward.

Just as Du Yiming's father hesitated, Meng Haiyun suddenly exclaimed, "Grandpa!"

Through a small window, everyone saw a figure staggering towards the well.

"We can't let a man close to eighty go to such a dangerous place!" Du Lang said as he quickly put on a gas mask and rushed out, leaving behind a sentence, "Stay here and don't move, don't cause any trouble. Don't worry, I'll definitely bring your grandfather back safely!"

Just as he caught up with Meng Qingshan and grabbed him, someone shouted loudly, "Danger, retreat!"

The tongue of fire gushed out of the wellhead, rushing towards the rescue vehicle convoy as if it wanted to devour everything around it.

Fortunately, the drivers had already run to a safe area. They knew it would be dangerous due to the high temperature at the wellhead. If this continued, it would explode.

Everything happened too fast, as if a tsunami had instantly swallowed the coastline.

Meng Haiyun's phone rang, and no one expected to get a signal at this time. The ringtone was like winter frost suddenly thrown around her neck, making her shudder.

She answered the phone, and it was Du Yiming. Despite the situation, Du Yiming was still laid-back, asking how things were on the mountain and urging her to come down early, saying she and Yu Junying would wait for her to return to Dunhuang together. She also mentioned that the members of the rescue team had already gone up the mountain. Before going up, her mother specifically consulted experts, saying that there was almost no wind today, and hydrogen sulfide would gather in the well, but whether it would spread to the foot of the mountain depended on the wind direction and wind speed.

At that moment, there was a loud bang as the tire of the

leading truck exploded.

The ground trembled where everyone was standing, and it felt like the earth was tilting in an instant. The airwave carried dust, engulfing Du Lang and Meng Qingshan in an instant.

To prevent the fire from spreading, the mud from several other vehicles sprayed out like a flood and pressed down on the flames. The flames were extinguished wave by wave, but they were relentless, turning back to find new combustibles. So the fire burned up again in rounds, looking like a huge rolling cylinder from a distance.

Du Yiming's phone was still connected, and she heard the explosion very clearly. Her heart was about to jump out of her chest, and she shouted frantically like calling a lost soul, "Who, who is missing? Is it my dad?"

It took a long time for Meng Haiyun's eyes to focus again. She sawDu Lang shielding her grandfather as they fell to the ground together, like a suddenly deflated sack.

Without hesitation, she hung up on Du Yiming's call and dialed her grandfather's number.

Meng Haiyun's heart made a sound like a leaking balloon—puff, puff, puff ...

Then, the hearts of everyone present made the same sound.

Puff—self-blame.

Puff—guilt.

Puff—worry.

Puff—fear.

The ringtone of the phones was the collection and echo of these heartbeats. With each trembling and urging ringtone, Meng Qingshan finally moved a bit. He fumbled in his pocket and took out his old-fashioned phone, pressed the answer key, and said, "Hello, Haiyun, are you okay? There was a fire just now."

Hearing this "Haiyun", Meng Haiyunburst into tears.

Yes, Grandpa's memory is a maze. For so long, his address to Meng Haiyun changed with the changes in his memory route, always twisting and turning. This time, it was a straight line between them. His memory went straight to recognizing and remembering her as his granddaughter, not his aged wife or Jiang Juan. Moreover, all he could think about was his granddaughter's safety, without even a thought for himself.

"Grandpa, I'm okay. Why did you suddenly collapse? Are you injured? Is the gas mask damaged?"

"The car with the burst tire was only fifty metres away from the vent. When I walked over, the fire suddenly flared up. I was afraid it would engulf me, so I stepped back, but I stumbled over a stone. Did the other cars drive away? If they didn't, they might have been roasted."

Meng Qingshan was fine; he was still lucid, very lucid!

"They drove away, they all drove away! The other cars were relatively far away, so they're all fine. The driver wasn't injured either. Grandpa, how about you?"

"I'm fine, just a few minor injuries. Oh, there's someone else here."

Du Lang was just holding onto Meng Qingshan, but he didn't expect this old man to be quite strong and pulled him down. He felt the ground was also burned hot. Meng Qingshan was gesturing while seeming to say something. It seemed that the old man had forgotten about being stopped by him just now after being pushed around by the heat wave, but he didn't have time to explain. There were more urgent matters on the well. He instructed the old man to stay in place and wait for rescue while he rushed to the well.

The oilfield rescue team arrived quickly, and Meng Haiyun saw the fully armed rescue personnel carrying her grandfather down on a stretcher.

Meng Haiyun hurriedly rushed up, "Grandpa, Grandpa, let me see, how are you?"

She saw scrapes on her grandfather's hands and legs from falling to the ground, and even his pants were torn. How painful it must be!

The nurse was putting a breathing mask on his face. Before the thing that looked hard and uncomfortable was put on, suddenly, Meng Qingshan desperately pushed away the nurse's hand and said, "You tell them, 'Zeng Sun Ring, Pig Leak.'"

"What? What?"

She wanted to ask carefully and comfort her grandfather, but the nurse pushed her away, accurately put the breathing mask on Meng Qingshan, and lifted him onto the ambulance.

"Why is there still a girl here? Take her down the mountain!"

Immediately, another rescue worker came over, picked up Meng Haiyun, and ran. She was carried away like a bag of potatoes.

5

Meng Haiyun was placed in the employee dormitory by the rescue workers, the building covered with plants.

She walked around, feeling a bit melancholic. How lively it used to be here! Nearby shops and noodle houses were bustling with business, with customers coming and going constantly. But now, this town was empty, like a pond drained of water, lifeless. And her heart, too, felt empty.

Suddenly, the phone rang. She answered, and the other party said mysteriously, "Guess who I am."

Footsteps sounded simultaneously. Meng Haiyun turned her head, only to see Du Yiming. Du Yiming was holding a phone, waving cheerfully at her. Yu Junying stood behind Du Yiming, holding a voice recorder in one hand and a power bank in the other. It was obvious she was charging the voice recorder. Upon closer inspection, Du Yiming also had a notebook and pen, as if they had just returned from an interview.

"Didn't you follow the others to evacuate?" Meng Haiyun asked.

Du Yiming shook her head, saying, "No, my family didn't

leave, my friends didn't leave, how could I leave? I have to live and die with them."

Yu Junying said, "Hey hey hey, can you change your lines? I'm still recording here."

Du Yiming turned around, grabbed a notebook, and tapped Yu Junying's head, saying, "Silly, you should turn off the voice recorder! If my mum hears what I just said, she'll scold me again for using the word 'death'!"

Yu Junying rolled her eyes, "Humph, why didn't you say so earlier! It's already recorded now."

"By the way, where's your mum?" Meng Haiyun asked.

"She's still interviewing. She's too busy alone, so she asked the two of us to help. When we heard you were sent down here, we sneaked away. Oh dear, we need to hurry back now, if my mum can't find us, she'll be worried!"

On the way back, Du Yiming asked Meng Haiyun about her grandfather. Meng Haiyun responded casually, but her mind was filled with the few words her grandfather said to her before he was taken away in an ambulance.

Zeng Sun Ring? Pig Leak? What does it mean?

Thinking about it, she couldn't help mumbling. Yu Junying couldn't help but say, "What are you mumbling about? What spoiled bamboo? What leaking pig?"

"I don't know! My grandfather said that. It's strange, he specifically told me these before he was taken to the ambulance.

I think it should be important information, but I don't understand at all!"

"Well, maybe he was just hungry. Bamboo and pigs."

Meng Haiyun thought to herself: No, he was wearing a breathing mask, how could he be thinking about food? Could it be related to the accident at the well?

She opened the search engine, entered all possible combinations of these words, and searched once, but found nothing. So she casually searched for the handling methods of similar accidents in oil wells. Among them, there was one clearly written: Positive Circulation, Plugging Leak.

Oh, right, it should be this. Grandpa probably was slurring his words at that time, that's why it sounded like "bamboo" and "pigs"!

She told this new discovery to Wang Hui, asking her to immediately call the well site, maybe these five words might be useful.

Originally, Well 336 of Lion was located in a hilly area, with steep mountains and difficult roads; there was only a single narrow road, inconvenient for vehicles to travel by. After the accident occurred, the engineering team urgently constructed a temporary road, so that engineering vehicles could directly drive up to assist the well site operation as soon as possible.

When Wang Hui called the well site and passed on those words, Du Lang said that what Meng Qingshan said was indeed the solution to the accident. They were already dealing with it this way at the moment.

Meng Haiyun typed frantically with her fingers, searching for information.

Positive Circulation Well Control is the process of pumping drilling fluid from the drill string into the wellbore, displacing the fluid in the wellbore, and circulating it upward to the wellhead through the annulus.

And Plugging Leak is to inject drilling fluid or cement slurry containing plugging materials into the wellbore to seal the leak points inside the well, achieve wellbore pressure containment, and stabilise the circulating drilling fluid level inside the well.

At this moment, beside the oil well, Du Lang was exerting all his strength to push the gate, accompanied by the collision of machinery, emitting a low roar from his throat.

"Captain, captain, you can't move the gate alone!" Everyone knew that when the pressure at the wellhead reached a certain level, one person simply couldn't move the gate.

"Captain, I'm here!"

"Captain, I'm also here!"

"One! Two!! Three!!!"

"One! Two!! Three!!!"

Five pairs of large hands simultaneously grabbed the gate, and everyone gritted their teeth, exerting all their strength, enduring the scorching heat and pungent smell of the fire.

The faces under the gas masks, with their hidden and resolute expressions, seemed to be frozen in this moment.

"Valves ... all set ... we can ... start the well pressure. First team, operate the valve group; second team, inspect the pipeline; third team, conduct on-site safety checks. Quick! Let's hurry up!"

Several minutes later ...

"Reporting to the captain, all preparations are in place. We are ready to begin the well pressure operation, please advise."

"Received, everyone is ready, commence the well pressure."

"Yes!"

The workers restrained their nervousness, shouting enthusiastically to encourage themselves.

The courage to overcome difficulties from five different sources converged, and the hands of five individuals seemed to belong to one person. When these hands combined, they became magical.

Hands above the wellhead changed and intertwined—entering, rotating, lifting, pressing down ... These pairs of hands held their own fate, the fate of their colleagues, and even the fate of more people not present but sharing the same hardships.

Finally—

"Well pressure successful, emergency resolved! The danger ... is completely eliminated!"

When Du Lang shouted these words, veins bulged on his neck, tears flowing down his pitch-black face, like transparent rivers, and flowing crystals.

Chapter Seven

Lenghu Town

1

The ambulance took a turn and headed towards Lenghu town.

At this moment, Mr. Yang was also driving, chasing after the ambulance in the direction of Lenghu.

"Isn't the ambulance going to Huatugou Hospital? Why is it heading towards Lenghu?" Mr. Yang asked.

Meng Haiyun had just got the news. Her grandfather had only received first aid and basic treatment in the ambulance. He was clamoring to go to Lenghu, fearing that once he entered the hospital, he wouldn't be able to leave.

The medical staff were in a dilemma, but after making a call and consulting with Meng Haiyun's father, they reluctantly agreed.

Mr. Yang said, "This old one is really causing trouble, treating the ambulance like a private car!"

Just then, Meng Haiyun's phone rang.

"Dad!" Meng Haiyun exclaimed. She had a lot to say to her father at this moment, but she didn't get to say much before turning to Mr. Yang. "Mr Yang, please drive to Lenghu

Cemetery. My dad said my grandfather wants to go there."

"Huh? Go to the cemetery? What for?"

"Well, my dad said Xiao Chanzhi was buried there, and my grandfather wants to pay a visit."

Mr. Yang sighed, "This old man cherishes his friendship and brotherhood with his partner!"

At this moment, Yu Junying's phone also rang. After listening to the caller for a while, she simply responded with an "okay" before hanging up.

Curious, Du Yiming turned to Yu Junying, "Who called? What did they say?"

Yu Junying leaned her head against the back seat, closed her eyes, and remained silent. Every time the car swayed, she swayed with it. She hugged her arms tightly against her chest, as if she was holding onto a secret, fearing it would be ruined by the car's movements.

"Why are you holding back from me," Du Yiming interjected, "If you don't want to talk, then don't."

After a while, when everyone in the car had fallen asleep, Yu Junying muttered, "She's coming back."

Du Yiming instantly opened his eyes, "Who's coming back?"

" My Mum. She said she's not going this time."

"Isn't your mum a flight attendant? Flying up in the sky all the time, how great is that! Can she bear togive up this job?

Must be just teasing you," joked Mr. Yang.

"My mum never teases me! She never has. If she says so, she definitely will!"

"So why is she suddenly coming back?" asked Du Yiming.

Yu Junying covered her face with both hands. Du Yiming pulled her, asking, "What's wrong? Why are you crying?"

"Who's crying?" Yu Junying spread her hands. Indeed, there were no tears on her face; instead, there was an uncontrollable smile at the corners of her lips and cheeks.

"So, this is laughter?"

"My mum heard about the incident at Huatugou and got scared. She said she'd rather earn less money than be away from me. Without me, she said her life would lose meaning." Yu Junying paused, her eyes half-lidded. "It's the first time my mum has said something like this."

"Oh my, our Ying is blushing."

Meng Haiyun seemed to witness a crack in Yu Junying's once rigid exterior, revealing a gentle warmth. Perhaps this was something she had been guarding all along, maybe even unbeknownst to herself. To prevent this warmth from fading, she enveloped it, hiding it away deep within.

It turns out, no matter how hard or thick the shell may be, there's always a key to unlock it. That key is the mother, the one who made Yu Junying shed her mask and open her heart. But for Meng Haiyun, her mother was already a kite drifting towards heaven, her grip on the increasingly blurred string tightening, yet the kite never returning. So, what about the shell in her heart? It equally confines her, leaving her no room to breathe.

"We're almost at Lenghu," Mr. Yang's voice interrupted Meng Haiyun's thoughts. She looked up, finding the scene before her strangely familiar, as if she had been here before.

Lenghu was on the way to Huatugou. After the town became ruins, it was unsightly to leave it exposed, so it was enclosed by a colourful fence. While driving by, people barely noticed it.

How could this be Lenghu? Lenghu was Grandpa's cherished land, a place Mum refused to mention. It should have a sign, whether warm or desolate, sufficient to reflect its uniqueness. When we yearn for a place, it's not just for its scenery but for the emotions intertwined with it. So, that place must be special enough, otherwise, we'd feel adrift. Whose attachment was the current Lenghu?

"Don't worry, it's still half an hour away from the cemetery," said Mr. Yang.

"Ah? Do we still have to drive that long?"

"Lenghu is vast, 17,000 square kilometres, even larger than Shanghai. Who'd have thought!"

The car resumed its journey on the bumpy road. After a while, a stone monument came into view. After days in the desert, everyone felt weary, so when a pristine white monument stood tall there, they were pleasantly surprised, as if finding an oasis in the desert.

Two vehicles were parked there, one was an ambulance carrying Meng Qingshan, the other was an off-road vehicle.

Where was Grandpa? Why couldn't she see him? Meng Haiyun anxiously searched through the car window, her trembling hand reaching for the door handle.

The door was pulled open, and she was immediately enveloped in a soft, warm hug.

Meng Peng's beard was unkempt, his wheat-coloured face adorned with numerous wrinkles up close, stained with dirt, like a piece of used, wrinkled dishcloth. This face was different from the fair, smooth face of Dad in her childhood dreams. Meng Haiyun refused to admit that there was a bit of imagination in her childhood memories. She could only sigh at how time and environment could reshape and refine a person into something entirely different.

Meng Haiyun took a deep breath. This sudden embrace, the embrace she had longed for, made her feel uneasy. It's strange, when one misses someone so much, but when that person stands in front of them, it feels like unfamiliarity takes over. Those longings floated away like bubbles.

She broke free from Meng Peng's embrace. To conceal any emotional turbulence, she deliberately looked around, asking, "I heard Grandpa also came, where is he?"

"Just thinking about your grandpa, don't you miss me?" Meng Peng patted Meng Haiyun's head. She felt the warmth flowing from Meng Peng's hand, a comfort more fitting than a hug.

"It's not that I don't miss you. Dad, what did the doctor say about Grandpa's injuries?"

"Just some minor external injuries, nothing to worry about. If it were serious, the doctor wouldn't have let him come to Lenghu first."

"So, where is he now?"

"There, look."

Meng Peng pointed with his hand, and Meng Qingshan was standing under the memorial monument in the martyrs' cemetery. There were no pines or cypresses surrounding the martyrs, only yellow sand accompanying them.

Meng Haiyun and her father walked over, only to hear Meng Qingshan murmuring to himself, "I want to go and see Chan Zhi, where is he?"

The sandstorm was too strong, many tombstones weathered, the words on them became unrecognizable. Those who left their final marks here were all oil workers, some sacrificed for oil, some left a will for their descendants to bury them here.

Meng Qingshan walked past every grave, gently touching

the tombstones, brushing away the dust, then carefully examining the mottled characters on them. Meng Haiyun followed Meng Qingshan, helping him identify the names on them. However, the cruelty of the plateau's wind and sand remained unchanged over the ages, ruthlessly eroding various marks of human existence. Over four hundred tombstones, standing silently in rows, silently upright, they were silent swords, leaning against Kunlun, pointing directly at the sky, heroic and majestic.

They searched through all the tombstones but found no tomb of Xiao Chanzhi. Meng Qingshan was unwilling to give up and decided to search again. On the second search, every time Meng Qingshan passed by a tombstone, he used his weathered hands to caress the both sides of the tombstone, as if embracing the departed unnamed heroes. To Meng Haiyun, it seemed that rather than saying her grandfather was searching for his dear comrade Xiao Chanzhi, it was more like he was bidding farewell to all his comrades, bidding farewell to their glorious years and youthful dreams.

As they walked out of the cemetery, Meng Haiyun picked up a handful of yellow sand and handed it to her grandfather. Fine sand flowed like water from his fingers, accompanied by the clear tears from the corners of his eyes.

They softly recited the couplet on the martyrs' cemetery:

Aspiring to find treasure in the desert, achievements accompany Qilian; Devoting to the oil industry, fame coexists with Kunlun.

They moved their steps lightly, fearing to disturb the people sleeping beneath the mountain.

The car drove towards the main road, the cemetery gradually receding. At a glance, the tombstones were neatly arranged, extending towards Kunlun Mountain. The mountain ranges spanned the desert, extending the endeavours, aspirations, and pursuits of people for a long time, overlapping the circles of life. And the drilling machines compressed life's experiences so narrow, so narrow that it became a small world, life and death were close, close enough to switch places in the blink of an eye.

"After I die, I want to be buried here." Grandfather said, then leaned against Meng Haiyun and fell asleep deeply.

2

Meng Qingshan seemed to have had a long dream, only now did he wake up as if from a dream. He looked carefully at Meng Haiyun, hoping he wouldn't make a mistake again, this was his granddaughter. Suddenly, a wave of guilt swept over him.

"I'm sorry, granddaughter, if your dad hadn't come back to take care of your grandmother at the time, if I hadn't kept persuading him to come back, maybe your mum wouldn't have separated from him. With your dad by her side, she might not have had the car accident, and you all..."

"Grandpa, you should get a good check-up in the hospital. When you come back home, you'll still have to teach me how to make liquorice pulp." Meng Haiyun grabbed her grandfather's hand, holding back her tears. Many times she angrily wanted to question her grandfather and father whether they felt guilty towards her and her mother. She imagined the scene where her father and grandfather were speechless when confronted with this question, but the apologies came when she didn't need them, leaving her flustered and aggrieved.

While the nurse was treating the wound, the doctor quietly told Meng Peng and Meng Haiyun, "His body hasn't suffered any major external injuries, but when I communicated with him just now, I asked him how he got injured, he seemed confused and couldn't explain clearly. I asked him some more questions, and his answers weren't very clear either. I preliminarily judged it as symptoms of Alzheimer's disease."

"Memory decline and some cognitive impairment may occur." Meng Haiyun interjected. Looking at her father who was looking at her suspiciously, she hurriedly added, "We checked, we, Auntie Xiao and I."

"Yes, sometimes they are emotionally unstable, and prone to talking to oneself. After you go back, you must take good care of the old man as much as possible, accompany him, make him happy, and delay the progression of the disease."

In the hospital corridor, Meng Haiyun briefly told her father about her and Xiao Ge finding out that her grandfather was sick, and later bringing him back to recall memories. Meng Peng touched Meng Haiyun's head and said, "Haiyun has grown up, it seems you can help dad take care of grandpa in the future. Sometimes old people are as capricious as children."

Coming out of the hospital, Meng Peng decided to take everyone to see his old home. Meng Qingshan was excited like a child and insisted on sitting in the front passenger seat to direct his son. When Meng Peng was about to reach the intersection, he pretended not to remember the way and asked Meng Qingshan whether to turn left or right. In the old man's increasingly confused mind, Lenghu was always the bright part. Here, he would never get lost, even if everything here had changed beyond recognition.

The home Meng Peng spoke of was now a pile of ruins.

For future generations to visit, Lenghu left behind a small part of the base's remains. The core area was only a crossroad of no more than two or three kilometres in any direction, which could be traversed in ten minutes.

Meng Peng confidently said that his former home was here.

The houses in front of them were either missing roofs or with broken walls, rows of openings, empty inside, like the mouth of an old man with missing teeth, wide open to reveal everything. There was no trace of the past prosperity! But now there was also natural beauty, the holes didn't matter, the blue sky came as patches, and the snowy mountains came as walls.

Meng Haiyun had always heard people say that the most widely spread saying in Qaidam was "No birds in the sky, no grass on the ground, stones run when the wind blows". She had heard this saying too many times, her ears were almost calloused. But when her father stood on the ruins, he sang a completely different song. Meng Haiyun felt that this song was the depiction of the real Qaidam.

The vast Gobi stretches endlessly,
Kunlun Mountains hanging in the clouds.
The silver-edged Gats Lake,
Reflecting the azure sky in its waters.

Where is there such a wonderful place?
Our Qaidam is like a painting.

The Yellow River and the Yangtze River originate
from Kunlun,
The drilling rigs in Qaidam are as dense as forests.
Oilseedlings cover the ground like spring grass,
The wind blows, and the smell of oil permeates the
air.

In such a rich place, where else could it be?
Our Qaidam is a treasure trove.

"Dad, what song is this?"

"It's called 'A Little Song of Qaidam.' All the children of our generation in the oilfield know it. Sounds nice, doesn't it?"

"It's lovely, really lovely. Teach me when you have time."

Meng Qingshan's face flushed, humming softly on the side, "In such a rich place, where else could it be? Our Qaidam is a treasure trove."

There was a plaque standing beside the ruins. Du Yiming and Yu Junying had been to Huatugou a few times, but this was their first visit to Lenghu. They were curious about every piece of writing they could find here and leaned over to take a look.

Without listening to the narration, it's hard to believe that there used to be administrative buildings, residential areas, gas stations, and small shops here, where tens of thousands of people lived. Life wasn't just a few words on a narration; life was fuel, rice, oil, salt, and the memories and imprints of a generation or even generations. But life could also be rough and involuntary. Tens of thousands of people moved away because of oil depletion, but there were still some things that couldn't be blown away or wiped off. What Meng Haiyun wanted to see was precisely this part.

Meng Peng suddenly ran to a distant mound and struck a pose as if gazing into the distance, saying, "It's here, our home used to be here."

"There's a cinema here, and there's a bookstore over there," Meng Qingshan pointed to rows of dilapidated houses with exposed iron pipes and steel bars.

His eyes swept back and forth on the street, as if he could still catch a glimpse of the past.

Lenghu was the unique home of the descendants of the oilfield, and their childhood, though difficult, was also filled with fun, rolling iron hoops, kneefighting, playing with beanbags ... going to the canteen with siblings to get food, sitting on small stools to watch open-air movies, carrying water home with a big stick. The crude oil at the doorstep was their coal pile. When it got cold, it would solidify and could be taken down and thrown into the stove to burn. When it got hot, after being exposed to the sun, it would turn back into crude oil.

People often despise what they are used to. He hated being born in such a place when he was a child, vowing to go to places with more water and trees when he grew up, to escape the sandstorms, to escape the pungent smell of oil. Later, he did exactly that.

Every year, Meng Qingshan would say the same thing: "The oilfield is recruiting. Shall I sign you up?"

"I'm not going!"

"Don't you miss home?"

"No!"

At some point, when he said he wouldn't go or didn't want to, he began to hesitate and waver. Most of his classmates and relatives worked in the oilfield system. He wore short sleeves and shorts in Hainan, while others wore thick overalls. He sent pictures of the Remotest Corners of the Globe, a landscape of Hainan, and they sent pictures of oil wells.

What really made him consider returning to the oilfield were his parents, who grew olderin the oilfield, the very place he was born. Although he didn't want to leave the outside world, he decided to go back. It was his family mission, already engraved in his genes.

After experiencing the wonders outside, and then coming back, they would have fewer regrets, but more determination. There were several oilfield second generations around him who were like him, choosing various professions, hoping to escape the identity of an oilfield person, but as they went along, they suddenly took a turn and went back.

At this moment, Yu Junying suddenly asked, "Lenghu, Lenghu ... it's strange, why is it called Lenghu?"

Meng Peng smiled and said nothing, turning to ask Mr. Yang, "Sir, shall we take them for a drive to the water?"

There really was a lake in Lenghu! It's just that the lake stood on the desert, like pieces of broken glass in a meadow. Seasonal flows alternately eroded the dried river channels, forming a network of intersecting gullies.

The road and the mountains were brown, the lake was grey-blue, and the scattered camel thorns were ochre. The lake illuminated the barren land, shining with expansiveness, brightness, and elegance, like a painting by Van Gogh.

"Is this a saltwater lake or a freshwater lake?" Du Yiming vaguely saw fish swimming in the lake and wondered if her eyes were playing tricks on her, so she asked. Freshwater was scarce in the desert, and most lakes, although beautiful, had too high a salt content, making them dead lakes in the real sense, devoid of vegetation and waterfowl. But the lake before them didn't seem to be like that; life had already found a way to flourish.

"It's a freshwater lake. In Mongolian, it's called Hutong Nuer Lake, which means very cold water," Meng Peng said.

"So, Lenghu is really cold, and there's actually a lake?! I always thought it was just a name, something random," Du Yiming said.

3

Along the lake shore were quite a few people, some in red overalls, others in casual clothes. Some who cared about their appearance used the lake as a mirror, fixing their hair. They barely finished grooming when a bus arrived, prompting them to stand up hastily.

"The bus is here—"

Someone shouted, and people hurriedly gathered. They watched eagerly as the much-awaited bus rattled down the cobblestone road.

So, people quickly picked up their belongings from the ground, some tiptoed to get a better view, while others pulled out slips of paper from their pockets, detailing what they needed to buy, which restaurant to take the kids to, and what supplements to bring to relatives...

"Where is this bus coming from and where is it going?" Meng Haiyun asked.

When it came to the bus, Du Yiming was quite knowledgeable. Many classmates took this bus to the oil fields to visit their dads or mums. Du Yiming shook his head and said,

"This is the bus between Huatugou and Dunhuang, a shuttle route serviceprovided by the oil fields for the convenience of workers. People going up and down meet here, many couples can only exchange a few words when switching shifts, then they have to say goodbye."

"Your mum, being a sentimental intellectual, loves to report on this scene. She even gave it a name, calling it the 'Kiss of Lenghu,'" Yang added.

"Where's the real kiss? My mum is just a romantic. But you wait and see, they won't even hug, just exchange a few words about home, swap keys, and that's it."

"Not romantic at all!" Yue Junying pouted.

Meng Haiyun found it amusing. She hadn't expected someone like Yu Junying, who seemed like a typical boy, to still have a girlish heart.

A worker in red overalls nearby listened to their conversation and chuckled, "We have beenmarried for so many years, how can it still be romantic?"

Meng Peng offered a cigarette, "You're in a hurry to get home to see your child, aren't you?"

The worker waved his hand to say "no" to the cigarette. Working in the oil fields for so long, he was afraid of any open flames.

"Yeah, we relay and take turns to care for the child. I work in Oil Plant 1, and she works in Oil Plant 3. Two months on, two months off, totally exhausted, where's the romance in that?"

The arriving bus seemed to have encountered some problem, it stalled halfway, while the departing bus was about to leave. The worker in red overalls called his wife on the arriving bus, "What's wrong with your bus? Are you close? Oh, my bus is about to leave, if you don't arrive soon, we might miss each other."

The departing bus was about to start, the driver shouting at those who hadn't boarded yet to hurry up.

"Just a little more time, couldn't you wait? You two won't be able to see each other this time, will you?" Meng Peng felt sorry for him.

"Sigh, it's not the first time. We often just miss each other this way. She's on that bus, I'm on this one. I know she's here, but I can't see her."

The man made the call, reminding his wife to stay safe, then hung up.

"Shouldn't youtalk about something else?" Meng Peng asked.

"With so many people on the bus, what else can we say?"

The man climbed onto the bus, found a seat, and dozed off.

Although the arriving bus was late, it finally arrived, and the departing bus started moving. The worker in red overalls quickly got up and leaned towards the window, hoping to spot his wife as the two buses passed each other.

He wasn't sitting by the window, so he had to bend over to peer out, his head tilted, forehead pressed against the window frame, his wrinkles folding like origami.

It seemed like his eyes weren't enough for the searching, so they had to lend him theirs. Meng Peng and the three girls also searched the opposite bus, even though they didn't know whom they were looking for, it didn't stop them from searching. Helping out was always enjoyable. Meng Qingshan stood by calmly, his gaze deep.

A pair of tender arms stretched out from the window, followed by a childish voice calling out, "Grandpa—Dad—Sister—"

Meng Qingshan felt a jolt, and Meng Haiyun, standing next to him, saw him sway slightly. Following the sound, she saw the two segments of tender arms being pulled in by adult hands, accompanied by a complaint, "How many times have I told you, don't stick your hands out!"

Meng Peng's gaze focused on the window where the arm extended, and he shouted loudly, "Tongtong, is that you?"

A childish voice from behind the car window replied, "It's me, Daddy!"

Even before the bus stopped, Meng Peng began banging on the door. As soon as the door opened, he and Meng Haiyun dashed against the flow of people getting off the bus and rushed to pick up Tongtong.

Tongtong hurriedly pushed him away, saying, "It's itchy!"

"Why are you here? Are you tired?"

"We were worried about you and Dad. Is he okay? Look at Haiyun, just a few days and she's already tanned." Xiao Ge said.

"Oh, there's nothing to worry about."

"I heard there was an accident at the well, and you happened to go up at this time. How can we not worry?"

This couple's daily conversation, which used to evoke mixed feelings in Meng Haiyun, had a different taste today.

She would also pay attention to me. She's just an ordinary, nagging mum. Dad wasn't snatched away by anyone. Meng Haiyun thought about many things.

On the car heading down, people became restless, clamoring for the driver to stop. Most of them had families on the bus coming towards them. It would be great even if they were allowed to get off the bus and say a few words with their families. The driver finally gave in and stopped the bus.

Meng Haiyun looked down at the lake, where the blue sky was perfectly reflected, calm and cool. If you drank it, it would surely send a shiver through your whole body.

Soon, the lake seemed to be filled with many water birds, countless legs paddling back and forth, but they quickly passed. Then two legs found another two legs and stuck together before stopping.

Meng Haiyun knew they were embracing. Just by looking at the reflection, she felt as if the people on both buses were connecting the lake water with their embraces.

The lake surface quickly filled up. The length and width of the lake determined how many shadows it could hold. Meng Haiyun didn't look up, but her eyes were also rippling. Why did she feel a bit faint and empty-hearted when she saw such a full lake?

She found herself staring at the shadows of three people, half on the lake and half under the lake, like neon lights, rippling. Meng Peng held Tongtong with one hand and Xiao Ge with the other. He was like an old hen, spreading his wings to protect the people in his arms. She also wanted to beg for a place in that embrace—yes, she regretted it. She regretted not cherishing it when the whole embrace belonged to her just now.

At this moment, she heard Meng Peng calling her, "Haiyun, come over here—"

She turned back and saw her dad extending an arm towards her.

"Come, Haiyun, come over here—"

Meng Haiyun returned to her dad's embrace, although she shared it with Xiao Ge and her sister, but she finally returned to this embrace.

She suddenly seemed to remember something and waved to her grandpa. Meng Qingshan quickly waved his hand, "I'm an old man, I won't meddle ..."

Meng Peng and Xiao Ge both laughed, saying together, "Come on, come on, you're the only one missing, it's rare for the whole family to gather in Lenghu."

Du Yiming and Yu Junying watched the family hug each other. Du Yiming said, "Hey, Lenghu is really nice, isn't it?"

"Indeed."

"I think Lenghu is good because Meng Haiyun might not leave anymore."

"Leave? Where was she planning to go in the first place?"

"When she first came, she kept saying she wanted to go back to Hainan to be with her grandma. Now she probably doesn't want to leave anymore."

Yu Junying cast a casual glance towards them, saying in a tone extremely incompatible with her age, "Hmph, it's not that simple, but I think this will be a very good start!"

Meng Haiyun looked up at Xiao Ge, nestled in her dad's embrace. Under her jet-black hair, a pair of bright eyes were looking at her.

With his arms open, her dad formed a semi-circle, splitting it between Xiao Ge and Meng Haiyun, with Tongtong's arms winding like vines around his neck. And Meng Qingshan was another, even larger semi-circle, trying to hold them as much as possible from across Meng Peng, looking somewhat comical.

Xiao Ge suddenly wriggled out of Meng Peng's embrace,

bent down and picked up a shoebox from the ground, and handed it to Meng Haiyun, saying, "For you, your dad bought it specially on his business trip."

Meng Haiyun opened the shoebox and found a pair of short boots similar to those worn by Du Yiming and her friends.

"It's her choice. She was afraid you wouldn't like them, so she said I bought them, but actually, she was worried you'd blame her," whispered Meng Peng to Meng Haiyun, winking discreetly.

Ah, Meng Haiyun, who was usually quite eloquent, suddenly became tongue-tied: "Auntie, um, I'll cook for you when I go home tomorrow. How about I make noodles for you? I'll make the soup noodles that grandpa loves."

"Ah, don't you dislike eating noodles?"

"It's not that I dislike eating them, it's just that I've never had delicious ones before. The noodles here are so delicious. I snuck into the noodle shop's kitchen and peeked a couple of times, then learned how to make them, heh heh."

Xiao Ge finally breathed a sigh of relief and smiled.

"I have a decision to tell you guys." Meng Haiyun suddenly jumped in front of Yu Junying and Du Yiming, speaking solemnly.

"Isn't it that you decided to go back to Hainan to open a noodle shop when you grow up? " Yu Junying joked.

Du Yiming was drinking water and almost sprayed it out.

With his arms open, her dad formed a semi-circle, splitting it between Xiao Ge and Meng Haiyun, with Tongtong's arms winding like vines around his neck. And Meng Qingshan was another, even larger semi-circle, trying to hold them as much as possible from across Meng Peng, looking somewhat comical.

"Guess."

The shift handover buses started again, and the people on the buses were either looking at the oilfield's wechat official account or chatting quietly. Two videos caused a stir.

One was Old Yuan, who was live-streaming on Douyin. The wind in Kazi was always strong. He wore a hat with two ears on top, and outside his red work clothes, he wore a military overcoat. It wasn't even mid-autumn yet, but the temperature in the work area was already freezing.

Old Yuan said, "Son, Mid-Autumn Festival is coming soon, and Dad won't be able to go home again. I want to say a few words to you ... Over all these years, I felt most sorry to you..."

He thought, ever since his son was a child, he hadn't been there for him. When his son grew up and seriously asked him for something for the first time, he couldn't fulfill his request.

He couldn't continue speaking, turned his head away, and buried his face behind the thick ears of his hat.

The other video was of a little fox in Kazi where Yu Yi stayed.

People who knew about the previous fox crowded around to look at the phone. The new fox had the same bright eyes, yellow fur, and a lithe and soft body like a wildcat. Its paws moved smoothly when running and were placed in front when still. Behind it, there was a large fox chasing after Yu Junying's car.

People speculated that the two foxes were actually a mother and child, with the big fox being the mother of the little fox. When the big fox went down the mountain to find food, it always ate a little for itself and hid most of it, probably for the child to eat.

"Our oilfield is getting better and better!" People exclaimed one after another.

As thebuses gradually moved away, the people by the lake were still huddled together.

Behind them, the huge mountains rose and fell, and the wind on the Silk Road made the sound of silk being torn.